JourneyThrough®

# Amos

30 Biblical Insights by **J.R. Hudberg**

*Journey Through Amos*
© 2019 by J.R. Hudberg
Published by Discovery House Publishing Singapore Pte. Ltd.
All rights reserved.

Discovery House Publishing™ is affiliated
with Our Daily Bread Ministries Asia Ltd.

Requests for permission to quote
from this book should be directed to:

Permissions Department
Our Daily Bread Publishing
P.O. Box 3566
Grand Rapids, MI 49501

Or contact us by email at
permissionsdept@odb.org



Design by Joshua Tan
Typeset by Lidya Jap

ISBN 978-981-14-7983-0

# Foreword

When I first read the book of Amos in my first year of Bible college, it left
a strong impression on me. The prophet Amos was heavy on the accusations
and discipline, and seemed to lack the hope that other prophets offered.
I left the book feeling anxious and somewhat depressed by the message that
there was no getting away from sin and judgment.

That was more than 20 years ago. I've come back to Amos a few times since.
He's still heavy, and his message still hits hard. But if we listen carefully to
what he says to the people of Israel, we can hear both the love and plan of
God. With vivid imageries, God calls to His chosen people: Remember who
you are. Live out who you are. The dire warnings of coming judgment were
an urgent call to repentance. If Israel continues to pervert justice and take
advantage of the weak, its fate will be sealed.

As people of God on the other side of Jesus' death and resurrection, it's
tempting to see the book of Amos as just a season in Israel's history. But
we do so to our own loss. Amos' message to Israel reverberates across the
centuries to touch our lives with its relevance. Jesus said, "From everyone
who has been given much, much will be demanded" (Luke 12:48). That is the
message of Amos. He calls to us as he called to Israel: You are God's, you are
His people, live like it!

**J.R. Hudberg**

# We're glad you've decided to join us on a journey into a deeper relationship with Jesus Christ!

The *Journey Through* series is designed to help believers spend time with God in His Word, book by book. Each title is written by a faithful Bible teacher to help you read, reflect and apply God's Word, a little bit at a time. It's a great accompaniment to read alongside the Bible, digging deeper into God's Word. We trust the meditation on God's Word will draw you into a closer relationship with Him through our Lord and Saviour, Jesus Christ.

## How to use this resource

READ: After reading and reflecting on the Bible verses, use the explanatory notes to help you understand the Scriptures in fresh ways.

REFLECT: Use the questions to consider how you could respond to God and His Word, letting Him change you from the inside out.

RECORD: Jot down your thoughts and responses in the space provided to keep a diary of your journey with the Lord.

# An Overview

Amos begins his prophetic career during the reigns of Uzziah in Judah and Jeroboam II in Israel by calling out the sins of Israel's neighbours. As he travels from the southern to the northern kingdom of Israel, he declares seven times that the fire of the Lord will descend and destroy the people around Israel. But Amos' final and most critical accusation springs like a trap on Israel herself.

In a series of speeches, Amos broadcasts God's evaluation of Israel's society and religious practices. He exposes their social injustices and religious formalism. Their indifference to the poor and their perversion of justice has filled the cup, and now it must be drained, right down to the dregs. Judgment is coming.

Following these speeches, which receive an unsurprisingly cold reception from the people of Israel, Amos is exiled back to Judah. There, he receives a series of visions about the future of Israel. They show him just how far Israel truly is from the Lord's standards. Through various images, the Lord shows Amos the coming punishment and fate of the people of Israel. In God's eyes, they have acted no different from the other nations. Of all people, they should have known better. Therefore, discipline is coming. But even when hope seems lost, God speaks of restoration. After the judgment, He will again plant His people in their own land.

## The Structure of Amos

| 1:1–2:16 | Charges against the nations, Judah, and Israel |
| 3:1–6:14 | Speeches of judgment against God's chosen people |
| 7:1–9:15 | Visions of discipline and restoration |

## Key Verse

Hear this word, people of Israel, the word the Lord has spoken against you—against the whole family I brought up out of Egypt: "You only have I chosen of all the families of the earth; therefore I will punish you for all your sins."
—Amos 3:1–2

# **Day** 1



Have you ever heard a lion roar? Perhaps at the zoo or the circus? It's an unnerving sound, even from the safety of the enclosure. Maybe it's the visuals that go with it—like the teeth in that open maw—that chill the spine and evoke fear.

Imagine hearing a lion roar on the open plains. No glass or bars separating you from those claws and fangs. That's the image that the book of Amos opens with.

Amos begins, as many of the prophetic books do, with the introduction of the book's writer (Amos 1:1). He is a southerner (Tekoa was just a bit south of Jerusalem) who has been sent to prophesy to the northern 10 tribes. It's a tough assignment: Israel and Judah were separate kingdoms at this point, and though they were all descendants of Abraham, the family connection was very loose in Amos' day. But Amos obeys, and travels north during the reigns of Uzziah in the south and Jeroboam II in the north (v. 1). That was sometime between 767 BC and 753 BC, a time of relative prosperity for the northern kingdom—but prosperity doesn't mean God's blessing. Amos' journey and message will be proof of that.

The first words Amos utters paint a picture of what is to come. The LORD doesn't just speak; He "roars from Zion and thunders from Jerusalem" (v. 2). The effect is catastrophic: the power of Yahweh's voice dries up everything from the fertile plains to the top of the lush mountain (v. 2). This is a picture of judgment, the imagery of destruction and difficulty.

It's important to note the place from which Yahweh's powerful voice comes. In this poetic couplet, Zion and Jerusalem are synonymous. They refer to the same place: the temple that stood in Jerusalem in the south, where God had established true worship. This verse would thus have been an initial criticism of the religion of the north, emphasising that the Israelites were not worshipping God in the way they were supposed to. When Israel split into the northern and southern kingdoms, temples were built in Bethel and Dan (see 1 Kings 12:25–33). But, unlike the temple in Jerusalem, these places of worship were, in reality, places of idolatry. The "sins of Jeroboam" (see 1 Kings 14:16, 16:31; 2 Kings 3:3) were one of the major reasons why Israel was taken into exile. False worship is one of the sins Amos comes back to again and again in his message to Israel.

But it's the power of God's voice that arrests our attention in these opening verses. Israel—and we—

have to reckon with the fact that when God speaks, things happen. **There is power in the voice and message of the LORD, and it demands attention.** The question is, are we listening?

# Day 2



If you are a sports fan, cheering for your favourite team comes almost instinctively. Sometimes, cheering against the other team is part of that experience. That's likely how the first crowd that heard Amos' message would have responded.

As readers of the book of Amos, we get the benefit of the editorial setup. We know whom the message is intended for—"the vision . . . concerning Israel" (Amos 1:1). But when Amos arrives in the northern kingdom, all they hear is the prophecy, which starts at verse 2. And that message begins not with an evaluation of Israel, but by condemning her neighbours. There's no easier way to gather a crowd than to pronounce God's judgment on the enemies of your listeners.

Six of Israel's neighbours fall under the spotlight of the prophet as he begins his message. God's message through Amos to these nations all follow the same formula. Starting with the phrase, "For three sins of . . . even for four, I will not relent" (1:3, 6, 9, 11, 13; 2:1), Amos lists the actions of these nations that have brought about the pronouncement of God's punishment. Then the nations' punishment is laid out: the fire of God will come and destroy their strongholds (1:4–5, 7–8, 10, 12, 14–15; 2:2–3). Remember, this message is going to the people of Israel, not to the nations being judged. God is reminding the Israelites of a very important fact: He is the God of the whole world, not just Israel.

Just what have these nations done wrong? In each and every case, the accusation is that of violating the human rights of other nations.

We can read the list of sins and shake our heads. What they were doing to each other easily defies modern ethical sensibilities: expatriation of entire communities (1:6, 9), brutal torture (v. 3), pursuit for the sake of killing (v. 11), and killing the pregnant and unborn (v. 13).

**God is concerned about international affairs; He holds nations accountable for their actions.** While Israel had a direct revelation of God's expectations on how to treat each other and the nations around them, these verses show that God's expectations extend beyond Israel's borders. The nations should have known that their behaviour was a step too far.

Amos makes clear that God has expectations, and failing to meet them carries dire consequences. We often talk about what we should be doing; Amos stands alongside and nods his head, warning us that it better not be just talk.

# **Day** 3

**Read** Amos 2:4–5

We've all had a moment of literally or metaphorically slapping our forehead when we realise we've done or said something against our better judgment. We had information that should have shaped our actions and words, but did something that didn't line up with what we knew. We're not alone: it's been happening since the beginning of humanity, and the nation of Judah was no different.

After Amos recites the judgments coming on the nations that surround Israel, the Israelites' are likely to have responded with enthusiastic agreement. After all, these nations had mistreated their neighbours and God was punishing them for these abuses. It's interesting that many of the offences were not against Israel but against other nations; it reinforces the fact that God is the God of all the earth and that all nations are accountable to Him.

It's also significant that God is judging these nations even though they did not have His revelation and laws. God holds people responsible for what they know. The apostle Paul says something similar to the church in Rome (see Romans 2:12–16). Part of the point of Amos' judgment announcements is that all people know enough to be held accountable. **There is a law of humanity written on all hearts, and God holds people responsible for how they respond to it.**

In today's passage, we see that God's judgment (Amos 2:4–5) isn't just for other nations—Judah, too, is not exempt from responsibility! But instead of being judged for violations of human rights of their enemies or for war crimes, God's people are accused of rejecting the law of the LORD and worshipping false gods.

Amos uses the same framework for his accusation against Judah, his own people, that he uses for the other nations: "For three sins of . . . even for four, I will not relent . . . I will send fire on . . . that will consume . . ." (vv. 4–5). This literary pattern puts Judah on the same footing as the rest of the nations. Before God, Judah—the people of God who have received special revelation of His law—is just as accountable to God for her actions.

In fact, God's people may be held even more accountable because they have been given special and specific instructions about what is good and what is evil. As Jesus reminds us:

"From everyone who has been given much, much will be demanded; and from the one who has been entrusted with much, much more will be asked" (Luke 12:48).



God tells Judah that their own lies have led them astray from His commands (Amos 2:4 ESV). How might we make the same mistake of letting lies lead us astray from God's ways?

The people of Judah were accused of making the same mistakes as their ancestors. What are some ways you can positively learn from the past?

# **Day** 4

**Read** Amos 2:6–16

Have you ever watched a movie or read a book that ends with a twist, sometimes at the last moment? Whether it's a sudden switch in the setting or a character revelation, the surprise can change how you understand the entire story. That sudden and unexpected turn upsets what you thought you knew about where the plot was going.

A twist is probably a pretty gentle way of describing what happened with Amos' prophecy to the nation of Israel. As readers of the book of Amos, we've known since Amos 1:1 that Israel lay at the receiving end of this prophecy. But Amos' original listeners wouldn't have, as they would have only heard the speeches starting in 1:2, which addressed their surrounding nations. It would thus have been a complete surprise to hear the revelation of judgment turn to them.

Keeping with his established pattern ("For three sins of . . . , even for four, I will not relent", Amos 2:6), Amos sets his sights on Israel for the longest and most detailed accusation and discipline speech of the opening chapters. In fact, this turn towards Israel sets the stage for the rest of the book, which adds more specifics to the sins Israel committed and further elaborates the discipline God is sending on them.

Amos alternates between several key elements in his speech. First, he focuses on the sins of Israel (vv. 6–8). Then, he moves to God's acts of grace and provision for the people (vv. 9–11), before going back to their sins (v. 12), and ends with a description of the coming discipline (vv. 13–16).

As with the judgment of Judah, Israel's sins are not crimes of war against other nations. Instead, Israel is accused of committing atrocities against her own people. The force and the emphasis of this opening condemnation of Israel is that the powerful are dominating the weak, and that the rich are exploiting and abusing the poor (vv. 6–7). Justice is being perverted. **Over and over in the law, God's heart for the poor and the vulnerable is expressed** (see Exodus 22:22, 26; Leviticus 19:15; Deuteronomy 15:4, 11).

Amos reminds them that God had delivered them from oppression in Egypt (Amos 2:10), which makes their oppression of their own people all the more shocking. And the fact that they have silenced the prophets and made the Nazirites break their oaths (v. 12) suggests a deliberate and wilful ignoring of God's call back to faithfulness. Because of these things, God is sending judgment on them.

Amos is very explicit in the details concerning the judgment coming on Israel (vv. 13–16). These details combine to express the totality of the judgment. None in Israel will be able to escape the judgment.



God is not just concerned with correct beliefs, but also with correct behaviour (see James 2:14–26). Take some time to reflect on your actions and beliefs. How do they compare?

Through Amos, God condemns Israel's social structures and practices relating to the poor. How does your own society and culture treat the poor? What might Amos say to you?

# Day 5



It could be a buzz, a beep, or a ping: we all recognise the sounds our phones make to alert us to a new text from a friend or a news story from our preferred news site. We want to be constantly updated from certain sources, because they deliver information we care about. The sounds get our attention.

That's the effect of Amos' next statement to Israel in Amos 3. When Amos declares, "Hear this word" (v. 1), it was a summon to pay attention. No one listening would have ignored the notice that important information was being conveyed.

Though the statement (v. 2) is short, when combined with the introduction it covers a great deal of significant information.

This introduction to Amos 3 contains three very distinct and important elements: identity, relationship, and requirements. And they are all interconnected and dependent on each other.

First, it mentions Israel's identity. At the time that Amos prophesies, Israel and Judah are separate nations; they have been divided for some 150 years by this point. But God reminds the Israelites that they are still part of a larger group of people—"the whole family I brought up out of Egypt" (v. 1). This reference suggests that though they are politically separate, God still views Israel and Judah as a single people. It is an implicit indictment of their division.

This statement also reminds the people of their relationship to God, based on what God has done for them—delivering them from their slavery in Egypt.

This truth is stressed by God telling them that He has chosen them out of all the families of the earth (v. 2). This is significant; the words used imply an intimate knowledge. God knows Israel (not just the nation, but the whole family) deeply, and is closer to them than to any other people group on the earth.

**This choosing and knowledge, however, has certain necessary implications—there are requirements of those so chosen and known.**

Whenever we encounter a "therefore" in the Bible, we must always ask: What is it *there for*? In the case of Amos 3:2, the "therefore" signifies the implications of God's having chosen Israel. Because Israel is God's chosen, they must not sin against Him. When they do sin, breaking their side of the covenant,

God is bound by His covenant love to discipline them for those sins. The argument of the text contains a force of necessity. Because of the unique connection between God and Israel, it is His right and responsibility to discipline them for their sins.



Jesus' life, death, and resurrection put us in a special relationship with God. What does it mean to be part of a larger family of people who belong to God?

God's relationship to His people entails discipline when we have broken His requirements. In Hebrews 12:7, the author points to hardship as discipline and says that God is treating us as His children. How might seeing hardship as discipline change the way you respond to them?

# Day 6

**Read** Amos 3:3–8

For every action there is an equal and opposite reaction: this is one of the most basic lessons in physics. In the same way, everything has a cause—there is no reaction without action. With only one exception, everything (an event, occurrence, or movement) that has ever happened in the history of the universe has had a cause. Even the "causeless" event of creation had its true cause in the will and power of God.

This basic lesson is Amos' next argument (Amos 3:3–8). It's a sharp and strange turn from the preceding verses that announce that God has the right and responsibility to judge Israel's sins because of her relationship to Him. Why?

It is because Amos' message had taken a clear turn. He had begun by talking about God's evaluation and judgment of surrounding nations, but now he is talking about the sin and judgment of Israel. The former was easy to accept; the latter, less so. The reception of Amos' message would likely have soured, and the crowds listening to Amos would probably have turned from cheering to booing. They may even have begun to question his legitimacy as a prophet. Hence, he has to give them a lesson on cause and effect in verses 3–8.

In a series of questions, all of which show undeniable causes and each prompting the audience to answer "no" (the effect cannot happen without the cause), Amos defends his prophetic ministry to Israel. Using examples that are readily understandable to his audience— nature, hunting, and warfare— Amos leads them inexorably to his conclusion: "The Sovereign Lord has spoken—who can but prophesy?" (v. 8). His point, following the cause-and-effect reasoning of the previous verses (vv. 3–6), is that the effect (his prophecy) springs directly from its cause (God has spoken).

Amos makes it clear that he is not carrying out his mission for pleasure or profit. The Lord had revealed to him what was going to happen to Israel (1:1). As a responsible spokesperson for the Lord, he is compelled to deliver the message to His people.

In the New Testament, Peter also reinforces this prophetic necessity and responsibility when he declares that prophets spoke "as they were carried along by the Holy Spirit" (2 Peter 1:21). The prophets spoke because they were compelled by the Spirit; when God reveals himself, someone must speak.

What does this mean for us who read the Bible today? Scripture is God's self-revelation. It chronicles His works in the past, draws our attention to the life, death, and resurrection of Jesus, and speaks of God's kingdom coming to earth in its fullness. It is inspired by God and "breathed out" by the Spirit (2 Timothy 3:16); in a real sense, it is God speaking. **Do we who hear Scripture today have a prophetic responsibility?**



**Think**Through

Amos felt compelled to deliver the message that God revealed to him (Amos 3:8). What responsibility do we, as readers of the Bible, have in sharing the message with others?

Amos says the Lord causes disasters that come to cities (Amos 3:6). How do you understand this truth?

The Bible's message is one of hope, but there are parts that are difficult to read because they convict us of sin in our lives. How do you ensure that you are reading all of Scripture, and not just the palatable parts?

# Day 7



When we see a video, tweet, or meme that grabs our attention, we're likely to share it with our friends. They may then share it with their friends, and before you know it, it can "go viral". Some YouTube videos have been viewed more than 6 billion times!

While it's a stretch to call God's summoning of Ashdod and Egypt in Amos 3:9–12 "going viral", it is certainly an invitation to others to see something incredible. Unfortunately, in this instance, that incredible thing is the degeneration of Israelite society.

The surrounding pagan nations are called to witness the unrest and oppression that Israel is heaping on her own people. It gives us the impression that even the pagan nations can recognise that what is happening in Israel is wrong—while Israel herself remains blind to what transpires within her borders.

In Amos 2:6–7, the prophet accuses Israel of abusing the poor and the vulnerable. Now, he reinforces and clarifies this point, saying that they have plundered and looted (3:10). This taking of property from others and storing it up for themselves in their fortresses (v. 10) is different from taking spoils of war from an enemy. It is taking from their own people, divesting the poor of even the little they have.

So God announces their discipline with a "therefore" (v. 11), indicating that what will come is related to—or even caused by—what they did. This is a reminder of the principle of "what goes around comes around". **Jesus echoed this principle when He gave His hearers a similar warning against judging others, because, "with the measure you use, it will be measured to you"** (Matthew 7:2).

Ironically, Israel will be overrun by an enemy and the very thing they have done to their own people will happen to them. They, too, will be plundered, and the fortresses in which they stored the plunder taken from the Israelite poor will be demolished (Amos 3:11). Just as only pieces of a sheep are found after a lion has attacked it, only parts and shreds of people's homes will be left in the wake of this destruction (v. 12).

This picture has been interpreted as either the complete destruction of Israel or as the leaving of some portion of Israel. Both interpretations are possible and not mutually exclusive: there can be complete destruction, but God, in His grace and mercy, can preserve some. What is certain is that if Israel will not repent, punishment will come and it will be catastrophic.



Do you think God is still concerned about the exploitation of the poor today? How might the system in your country measure up?

One of Israel's sins was not loving their neighbour. Read the parable of the Good Samaritan (Luke 10:25–37). How might this understanding of who our neighbour is affect your interaction with the poor in your area?

# Day 8

**Read** Amos 3:13–15

The people of Israel were likely already frightened by Amos' message about Israel's sin and impending discipline. In Amos 3:8, he had warned: "The lion has roared— who will not fear?" It echoes the description of God in 1:2—as a lion whose roar dries up pastures and withers mountains. But God's message to Israel is not yet complete; there is more.

In 3:13–15, Amos begins to add more detail to the discipline that is coming to Israel. Two specific things will happen to Israel, both of which reflect a specific aspect of Israel's sin: improper worship (v. 14), and the decadence of the rich at the expense of the poor (v. 15). As with previous sins, the consequence fits the crime.

The altars at Bethel (v. 14) were places where sacrifices were offered to God (see Genesis 12:8, 31:13, 35:1). Adonijah and Joab also held onto the horns of the altar to escape death (see 1 Kings 1:50–51, 2:28). The thought was that no one would dare kill someone in the same place where sacred offerings were presented to the Lord.

So when the Lord says that He will cut off the horns of the altar (Amos 3:14), He is telling Israel that there will be no safe place when His judgment arrives. This is partly because Bethel had become an illegitimate place of worship. God had appointed only the temple in Jerusalem as the place of worship. But Jeroboam I established Bethel (and Dan) as places of worship, placed golden calves in the two sanctuaries, and ordained priesthoods to serve at these places (see 1 Kings 12:25–33). In destroying the altars in Bethel (13:1–5), God is sending a clear message that He is rejecting Bethel as a place of worship and that no place would be spared His discipline.

The destruction of the opulent winter and summer homes (Amos 3:15) may seem peripheral at first, but these homes were built from the dishonest gains of selling the poor and perverting justice (see 2:6–8). The fact that the elite in Israel could own multiple homes and mansions while others were being sold for owing a small amount of money was both a violation of the law and an affront to God, who cares for the vulnerable. The houses are symbolic of the sin in Israel, and so they will be destroyed.

## God is faithful and consistent.

And though there may be some time between the sin and its consequences—for He always gives people time to repent—He does impose the consequences for sin.

In the Old Testament, God prescribed specific places and practices to be followed in worship. What are some of your worship practices? How would you evaluate them?

While it is not wrong to be rich or successful, it is sinful when it is accomplished by taking advantage of others. How does this happen today, in individuals and in society? How can you respond to these kinds of abuses?

# Day 9



I used to watch a captivating television show called *Undercover Boss*. In each episode, the owner of a company would visit one of his or her branches to see how employees interacted with each other and with customers. Every episode ended with the big reveal of the boss' true identity, which would surprise all the workers.

Amos likes the surprise reveal, too. The prophet has already shocked his listeners by turning from pronouncing judgment on the surrounding nations to targeting Israel (Amos 2:6). But his next surprise will startle his audience even more.

Amos' next address is to the wives of Israel (4:1–3). He grabs their attention by calling them a cow (v. 1), a term of great insult and condemnation.

In a patriarchal society (one that is ruled by men), it would be unusual for a prophet to address the women. But Amos must do so, for the women have played an active role in the injustice and oppression in Israelite society, and are just as culpable as the men.

How are the women guilty? There are two possibilities. First, they may have been taking an active part in the oppression, perhaps by directly suggesting ways to take advantage of the poor. Second—and perhaps more likely, given the last phrase of verse 1, "Bring us some drinks!"— they may have been the ones demanding an opulent lifestyle and pushing their husbands to find ways to finance their desires. This idea is reinforced by the description of them as cows on Mount Samaria (v. 1)— that is, well fed on the lush grasses on the mountain.

These women are not spared the consequences of their sin. **God holds all people accountable for their part in an unjust society.** And their punishment is the most graphic of the book of Amos thus far.

Bible scholars are unsure whether the women being taken out through the holes in the wall (v. 3) are alive or dead. On the one hand, it could suggest that they are corpses that are grabbed by hooks (v. 2) and tossed out the holes. On the other hand, the warning of the women being cast out towards Harmon (v. 3) could also suggest a picture of exile, that they are taken away from their homes and led to another land.

What are some ways in which people may, knowingly or unknowingly, contribute to oppression?

God's justice sometimes feels delayed, but it will always come. How can knowing that God's justice is coming, shape how you pursue justice for yourself and for others now?

**Read** Amos 4:4–5

magine someone telling you that you are committing sin when you go to your local church, and that you are sinning all the more when you visit another church. This would be a shocking statement. How can we be sinning in our place of worship when we go to church to honour God?

Until this point in his prophecy to Israel, Amos' condemnation of their religious practices has been clear and obvious. He has pointed out that their places of worship are sinful and objectionable to God (see Amos 3:14). Now, the prophet begins to deepen his criticism, dissecting Israel's religious practices to reveal the rotten core.

In 4:4, Amos tells the Israelites that they are sinning simply by *going* to their places of worship in Bethel and Gilgal. These places represented a rejection of worship in Jerusalem. Worship at Bethel and Dan was idolatry because Jeroboam I had golden calves made and proclaimed them as Israel's gods there (1 Kings 12:25–33). Not only had he violated one of the Ten Commandments (Exodus 20:4), but he had also credited God's miraculous works to those idols (1 Kings 12:28, see also Matthew 12:22–37 about attributing the works of God to others).

But idolatry was not the only sin Israel was guilty of. Amos is also accusing the Israelites of having wrong motives and wrong hearts in their worship of God (Amos 4:5). While they were performing all the prescribed sacrifices, tithes, and offerings, the problem was that they were not doing these things in obedient response to God, but so that they could brag about them (v. 5). They loved to show everyone how religious they were.

There are many warnings about this approach to religion in the New Testament. In Matthew 6:1–18, for example, Jesus warned against doing good things for others to see and praying for others to hear. James, too, reinforces this focus on motives when he tells his readers that they do not receive from God what they are asking for because they are asking with wrong motives—so that they can "spend what you get on your pleasures" (James 4:3).

**Our motives for doing such things like giving, praying, and fasting are as important as the actions themselves.** God cares deeply about *why* we do something, not just *what* we do.

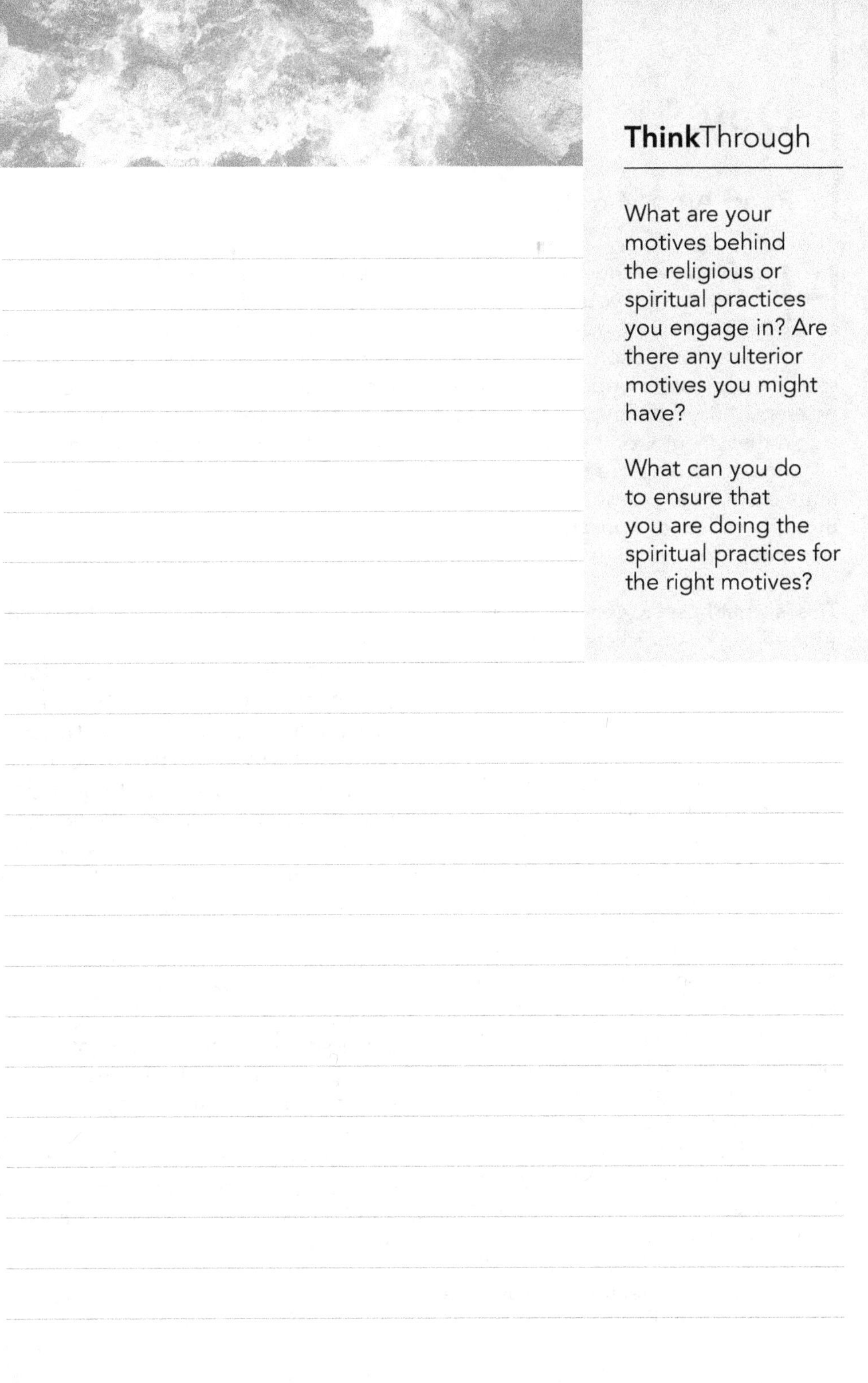


**Think**Through



What are your
motives behind
the religious or
spiritual practices
you engage in? Are
there any ulterior
motives you might
have?



What can you do
to ensure that
you are doing the
spiritual practices for
the right motives?

# Day 11

**Read** Amos 4:6–13

Have you ever tried to leave reminders for yourself? Like little signs or clues that were meant to represent something specific, such as an important lesson or event? I used to keep in my pocket a coin that my grandpa gave me, for instance, to remind me of a lesson that he once taught me. Sometimes, though, we forget what that symbol was meant to remind us of.

This is what has happened in Israel. In Amos 4:6–11, Amos lists six different events and circumstances that God had used to get the Israelites' attention: famine (v. 6), drought (v. 7), mildew and blight (v. 9), locusts (v. 9), plagues (v. 10), and war (v. 10). Yet, each of these reminders to Israel had the same result: "Yet you have not returned to me" (vv. 6–11), and they remained disobedient to God.

We may ask: How were these specific events supposed to remind people to return to God? In one sense, we know that it's in the middle of difficult circumstances that we naturally turn to God and cry out for His help. But, in this context, these events were more than random occurrences. They were terrible consequences directly tied to the curses of the law; each one was a specific punishment that God (see Deuteronomy 28:15–68; 32:23–27) would send on Israel if they broke the requirements of the covenant.

These events should thus have reminded the Israelites of the covenant and prompted them to repent and return to God. Individually and collectively, they should have reminded the people of their commitment to God and brought them back to covenant faithfulness.

While these events were indeed difficult circumstances, they were acts of mercy and grace, as they gave Israel one last chance to repent. **By allowing Israel to experience the consequences of her sin, God was mercifully warning them of worse punishment that would come if they did not repent.** But Israel still did not pay attention to the warnings, so they are now told: "Prepare to meet your God" (Amos 4:12).

As followers of Jesus today, we look forward to meeting God one day with great excitement and anticipation. But this would not have been the case for the Israelites of Amos' day. For them, the idea of meeting God would have been terrifying (see Exodus 20:18–19), for God would not be coming in rescue and salvation, but in judgment and punishment.

As if to reinforce the terrifying nature of a visitation from God, Amos proceeds to paint a picture of God's power (Amos 4:13). The God who "forms the mountains" and "creates the wind" can certainly come in judgment on His people.



How does God get our attention today? What can we do to make sure we don't miss His reminders to turn to Him?

How do you feel about the idea of God visiting you? Why?

# Day 12

**Read** Amos 5:1–3

Reading the prophetic books of the Old Testament can be a depressing experience. And reading about the sins that Israel is guilty of, and hearing of the punishments that God is going to visit on them, can be troubling. It can seem that humanity will never learn how to be faithful to God. It can also begin to seem like God is simply watching and waiting for an opportunity to punish His people.

But even though He has sent them His prophets with stark messages of warning, God does reveal His true heart for His people in the passages of Scripture that record His "laments" (Amos 5:1).

A lament is an expression of remorse and sorrow. Though Amos 5:2–3 describes Israel as fallen and never to rise again, God does not take delight in this situation caused by Israel's unfaithfulness. Instead, He mourns for fallen Israel.

This is the picture of a God who has warned His people, both in the past (by giving them the law with clearly-stated consequences for breaking the covenant) and in the present (by sending some disasters to call them to repentance). This is a God who has been patient with His wayward people, giving them ample opportunity to return to Him. And this is a God who grieves the discipline that is coming to His chosen people (see 3:2).

When the discipline comes, it is not because God's patience has been exhausted. Rather, it is a sign of His faithfulness to His word. In previous verses (4:6–12), God had reminded the people of His warnings and calls to repentance, but notes that they had not listened ("yet you have not returned to me", vv. 6, 8, 9, 10, 11). And this is why He is going to visit them in judgment. This is the result of their unfaithfulness: no one will lift the fallen Israel up (5:2), and only a tenth of the warriors that march out will return (v. 3).

Yet even in God's own faithfulness to His word and His covenant, there is lament and remorse that His people must suffer. He would much rather—as Jesus would invite people about 750 years later—that the weary and burdened come to Him to find rest (Matthew 11:28–30). **God's invitation to return does not have an expiry date; He is always willing to receive the repentant, that they may live** (see Ezekiel 18:23, 32; 33:11).

ThinkThrough

What impression or image have you had of God as a disciplinarian? How might today's reading change your view?

How can knowing how God feels about you change the way you live as His follower?

# Day 13

**Read** Amos 5:4–6

In the 2017 movie version of comic book heroine *Wonder Woman*, the superhero is given a sword called the "god-killer", which she believes can be used to kill an ancient enemy called Ares, the cause of humanity's strife and conflict. When she meets Ares, however, Wonder Woman is dismayed to find out that the sword fails to kill Ares. She had placed her faith and her hope in the wrong thing. In the end, she discovers that the real "god-killer" is Wonder Woman herself.

This is what Israel is being warned about in Amos 5:4–6, when they are told to seek God instead of going to the shrines in Bethel, Gilgal, and Beersheba. Much like how Wonder Woman put her faith in an object rather than in the person with the true power, the Israelites had thought that their salvation came from religious practice, and that doing the right things was the key to successful living.

God's response is to change their way of thinking by pointing them to himself. The LORD tells them that the religious places, and the rites they carry out at these locations, have no saving or life-giving power (v. 5). They will be destroyed and their power— whatever it was thought to be—will be revealed as nothing.

But there is more to God's plea to life than simply switching focus. Though Bethel, Gilgal, and Beersheba are idolatrous places of worship, God does not simply point them to Jerusalem, the proper place of worship. Instead, He instructs them to seek Him (v. 6). **It is a person—and not a place nor ritual—that brings life.** Israel had lost sight of God himself and was in danger; the answer to their plight was therefore to seek God. And those who seek Him will always find Him (see Jeremiah 29:13).

In the same way that God invited Israel to return to Him—and not to a location or ritual—Jesus pointed people to the true source of life. When the Pharisees rejected Him, He told them: "You study the Scriptures diligently because you think that in them you have eternal life. These are the very Scriptures that testify about me, yet you refuse to come to me to have life" (John 5:39–40). The Pharisees mistook the messenger for the message, the delivery system for the product. They knew the Bible, but they missed Jesus.

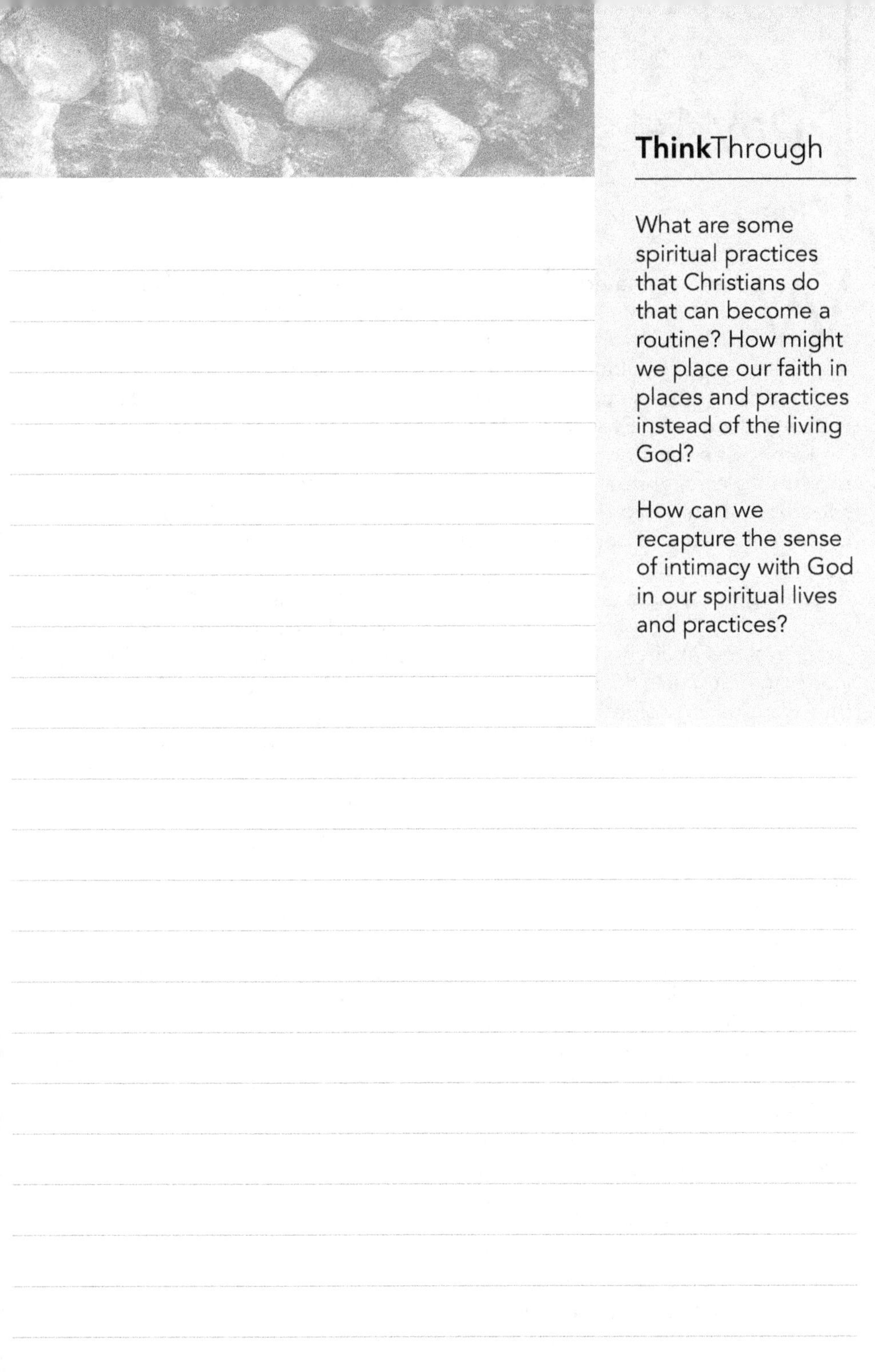

ThinkThrough

What are some
spiritual practices
that Christians do
that can become a
routine? How might
we place our faith in
places and practices
instead of the living
God?

How can we
recapture the sense
of intimacy with God
in our spiritual lives
and practices?

# Day 14

**Read** Amos 5:7–13

We are fascinated by things that turn into something completely different. For example, caterpillars into butterflies and moths, tadpoles into frogs, and coal into diamonds. Even in movies, we love to see transformation—robots into cars, normal people into superheroes, and bad guys having a change of heart and becoming good guys. It's amazing to see one thing becoming something else.

Israel had this ability to turn one thing into something else. Unfortunately, they were taking something good, valuable, and desirable and turning it into something bad.

In Amos 2:6–8, Amos accused Israel of perverting justice. Now, in 5:7–11, he gives more details on how they have ignored justice. In fact, he says, they have turned "justice into bitterness" (v. 7). Justice has become something that people no longer desire (v. 10), and the justice system in Israel has become so corrupt that the poor don't get justice in the courts (v. 12). In fact, those who need to use the courts would rather avoid them (v. 13). Rather than being a source of good in society, the legal system has been transformed by greed into bitterness (vv. 11–12). That is why Amos says these people have cast righteousness (behaving rightly and in good relationship with others)

"to the ground" (v, 7). It is a picture of contempt for righteousness.

In this section, Amos repeatedly introduces the sins of Israel (vv. 7, 10, 12) and follows with a description of the power of God and the coming consequences of her sins (vv. 8–9, 11–12). This pattern conveys the point that Israel is guilty, and God is powerful enough to discipline. **Israel should not doubt their guilt, the intention of God to discipline, nor His power and ability to carry it out.** The God who turns the night to day (v. 8) and destroys the stronghold and fortified city in a moment (v. 9) can easily topple a mansion (v. 11).

Again, the discipline that God will give is related to the sin that Israel has committed. The stone mansions were likely built with the dishonest gains taken from the poor using the corrupt legal system (v. 11). God will not allow Israel to enjoy the fruit of their dishonesty and corruption.

Reflect on your own personal sense of justice in the light of what the Bible says about it. How does it match up?

If you're asked, "Where is God in the midst of injustice?", how would you respond? How does today's passage address this question?

# Day 15



The idea of retribution was dominant in ancient Israel. The thinking was that if you did good things, God would bless you. Conversely, if you did evil things, God would punish you. In everyday life, this translated into the belief that if things were going well, you were doing what was right and God was pleased with you. But if things were going poorly or bad things happened, God must then be punishing you for some wrong thing you did.

This belief is taken directly from the blessings and curses laid out in the law by God himself. Deuteronomy 28 and 30 seem to support this way of thinking. Essentially, God had told Israel that if they obeyed the law, He would bless them, but if they sinned and broke the covenant, He would punish them with various curses.

At the time that Amos visited Israel, it was a prosperous time. They were safe from their enemies, and their economy was doing well. Because of this, they thought that God was pleased with them. The idea that they were sinning would have been unbelievable, if not entirely incomprehensible. Amos 5:14 expresses this line of thinking. As the prophet observes, the Israelites' likely response to Amos' prophecy was: "God is with us!"

Amos, however, rejects this thinking. His message, in part, is: prosperity does not imply God's pleasure. A nation can prosper while doing the wrong thing, but will eventually see judgment. But, Amos tells the Israelites, if you do what is good and hate what is evil, then God will really be with you—just as you say (v. 15).

Jesus encountered this same line of thinking in His day. In Luke 13:1–8, Jesus noted that suffering hardship and misfortune were not signs of guilt (vv. 2–3), while suggesting that freedom from hardship did not mean someone was innocent. He then urged His listeners to repent so that a similar judgment did not befall them (v. 5).

It is tempting and easy to believe that if we are good, moral, fair, and just, life should go well for us. **It's just as easy to believe that if life is going well, it means that we do not have anything to repent of.** What is your thinking about guilt and punishment today?

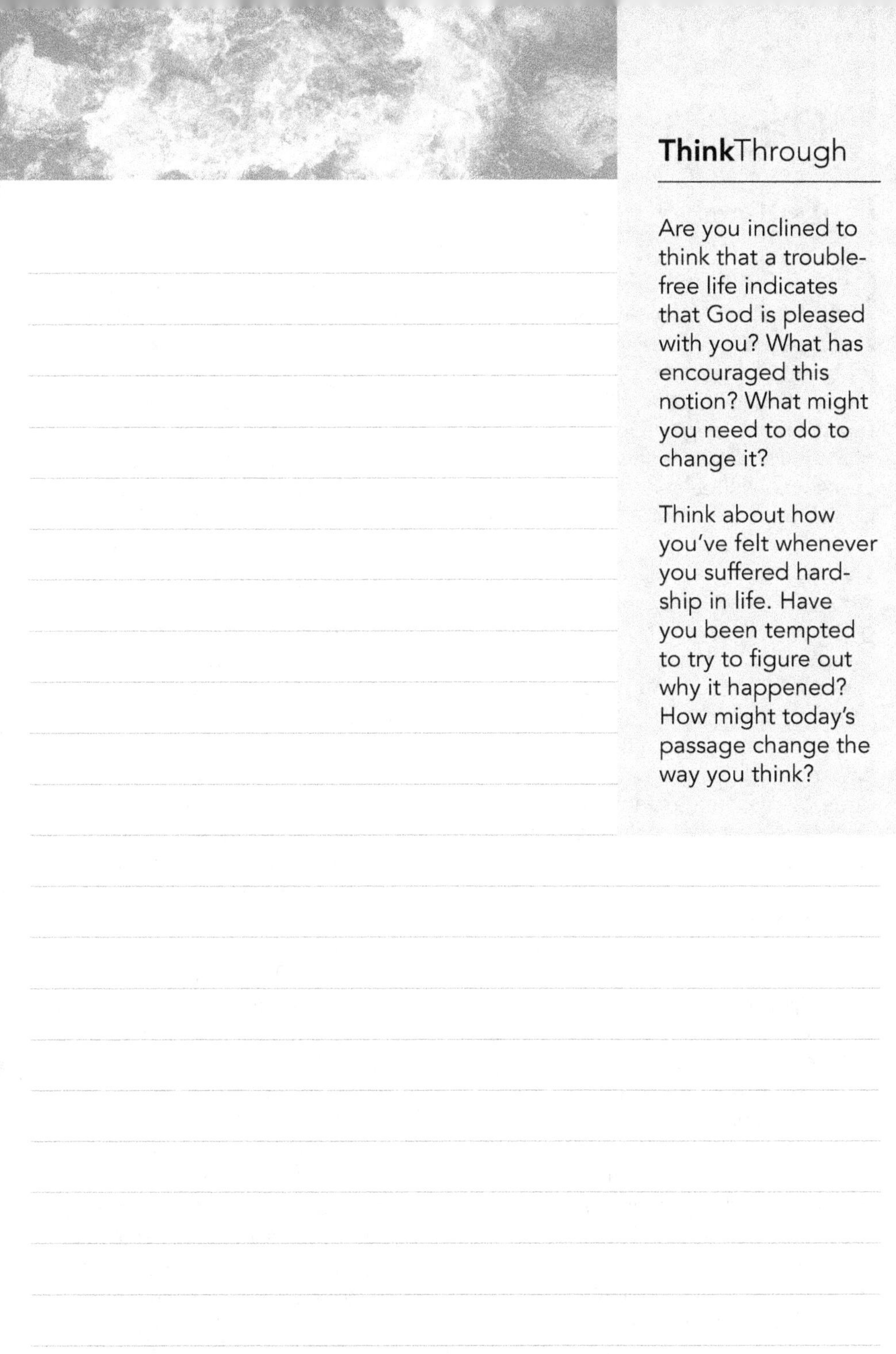



Are you inclined to think that a trouble-free life indicates that God is pleased with you? What has encouraged this notion? What might you need to do to change it?

Think about how you've felt whenever you suffered hardship in life. Have you been tempted to try to figure out why it happened? How might today's passage change the way you think?

# Day 16

**Read** Amos 5:18–20

I n Matthew 25:31–46, Jesus tells a story. It's not His typical parable nor is it exactly a clear prophecy. Rather, it is a startling picture of what the coming judgment will be like for those who belong to God and have a place in His kingdom (vv. 34–40), and those who will be sent away to eternal punishment (vv. 41–46).

The separation of sheep and goats catches all present by surprise. Both groups ask the same question about the criteria used to judge them: "When did we see you . . . and help (or not help)?" (vv. 37–39, 44) Jesus is teaching them that they have misunderstood and therefore misapplied what it means to be righteous. This scene of judgment is meant to correct a significant misperception about who would enter the kingdom of God and why.

Amos does a fair amount of theological correction in his messages to Israel. Here, he addresses the issue of "the day of the Lord" (Amos 5:18). In ancient Israel's theology, this was highly anticipated as God's ultimate blessing to Israel as His people. In their incomplete understanding, the day of the Lord represented the time when Israel would be victorious and dominant in all aspects of life, from social to economic to militaristic— when all of life would be perfect.

Amos seems to shake his head at this idea. You can almost hear him thinking, *Why do you think that the day of the Lord is going to be a good thing for you?* He tells the Israelites that it is going to be the exact opposite of what they expect. They are looking forward to light and life (v. 18), but Amos says that the day of the Lord will be darkness, "pitch-dark, without a ray of brightness" (v. 20)

This contrast of light and darkness sandwiches Amos' message of inevitable, unavoidable disaster (v. 19). Imagine that you were the person running for your life from the claws and jaws of a lion. You do so but your relief at escaping one terrible fate is short-lived, as the next predator, a bear, takes up the chase. Somehow, you miraculously escape the bear and make it to the safety of your home. Tired, you rest your hand on the wall, thinking that the worst is surely over . . . only to be bitten by a snake inside your own home. Your demise seems to be fated.

For the Israelites, says Amos, there is no escaping the day of the Lord. **It will be a day to be feared and not celebrated, because they have wrongly understood their position with the Lord.** Their chosen

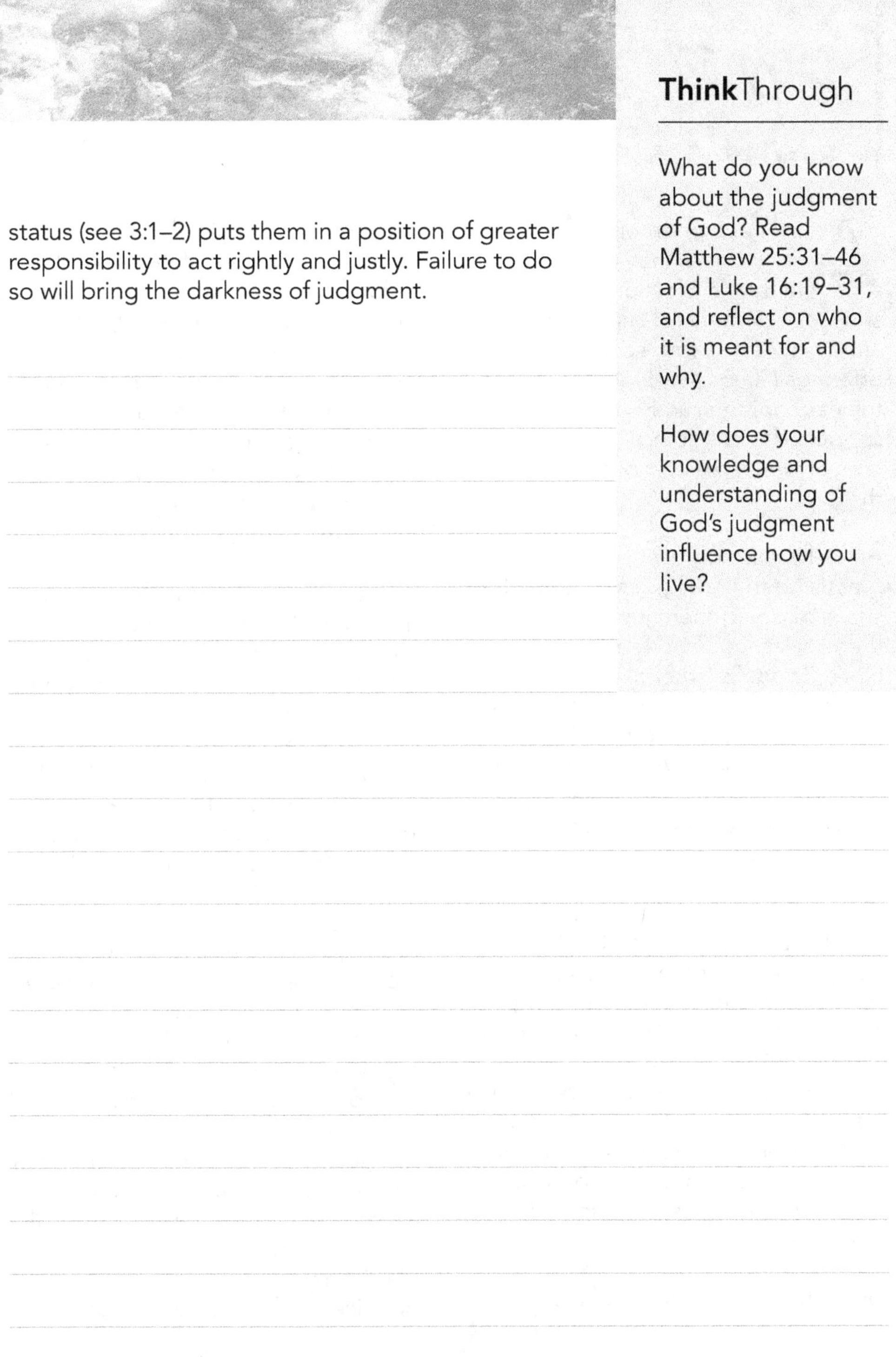

status (see 3:1–2) puts them in a position of greater responsibility to act rightly and justly. Failure to do so will bring the darkness of judgment.

# Day 17



As far as the Israelites are concerned, they have been faithful and religious. At the shrines in Bethel and Gilgal, they are worshipping with sacrifices and offerings (Amos 4:4–5). In their minds, they are doing exactly what they are supposed to be doing—following the laws of worship as set out by God in the law.

Amos has already accused Israel of practising their religious rites just for show, of doing them just to make themselves look and feel good (v. 5). Now, God tells Israel directly what He thinks of their religious practices. In case there was any doubt about what He said previously, Amos 5:21 makes it explicit: "I hate, I despise your religious festivals; your assemblies are a stench to me."

We might ask: Isn't there something good in at least part of what they are doing? Shouldn't they get *some* credit for keeping the festivals, bringing in their offerings, and singing the songs of worship? (vv. 21–23). Weren't the rituals themselves correct, even if they were carried out in the wrong place and for the wrong reasons? Yet it is not these faults to which God points when He expresses His disdain for their religious life.

Ultimately, God's loathing and rejection of the Israelites' worship is caused by their unjust society (v. 24). The twin attributes of justice and righteousness are what God desires of His people, not mere religious practices. This is a message that is repeated throughout Scripture: **God does not want obedience to a set of rules, but desires a heart that is devoted to Him and a life that is lived from that devotion.**

Religious practices do not make you right with God. In Matthew 9:13, Jesus quotes Hosea in telling His listeners that God desires mercy, not sacrifice. Several times Jesus accuses the Pharisees of ignoring the more significant matters of the law (like justice, mercy and faithfulness), while keeping some of the more minute points about tithing (for example, Luke 11:42).

In contrast, James lays out what it means to be truly religious: "Religion that God our Father accepts as pure and faultless is this: to look after orphans and widows in their distress and to keep oneself from being polluted by the world" (James 1:27). Religion is not about songs, offerings, and prayers. Rather, it is about how we care for one another, especially the vulnerable. If we are lacking in this area of life, then all our "correct" religious practices mean absolutely nothing.

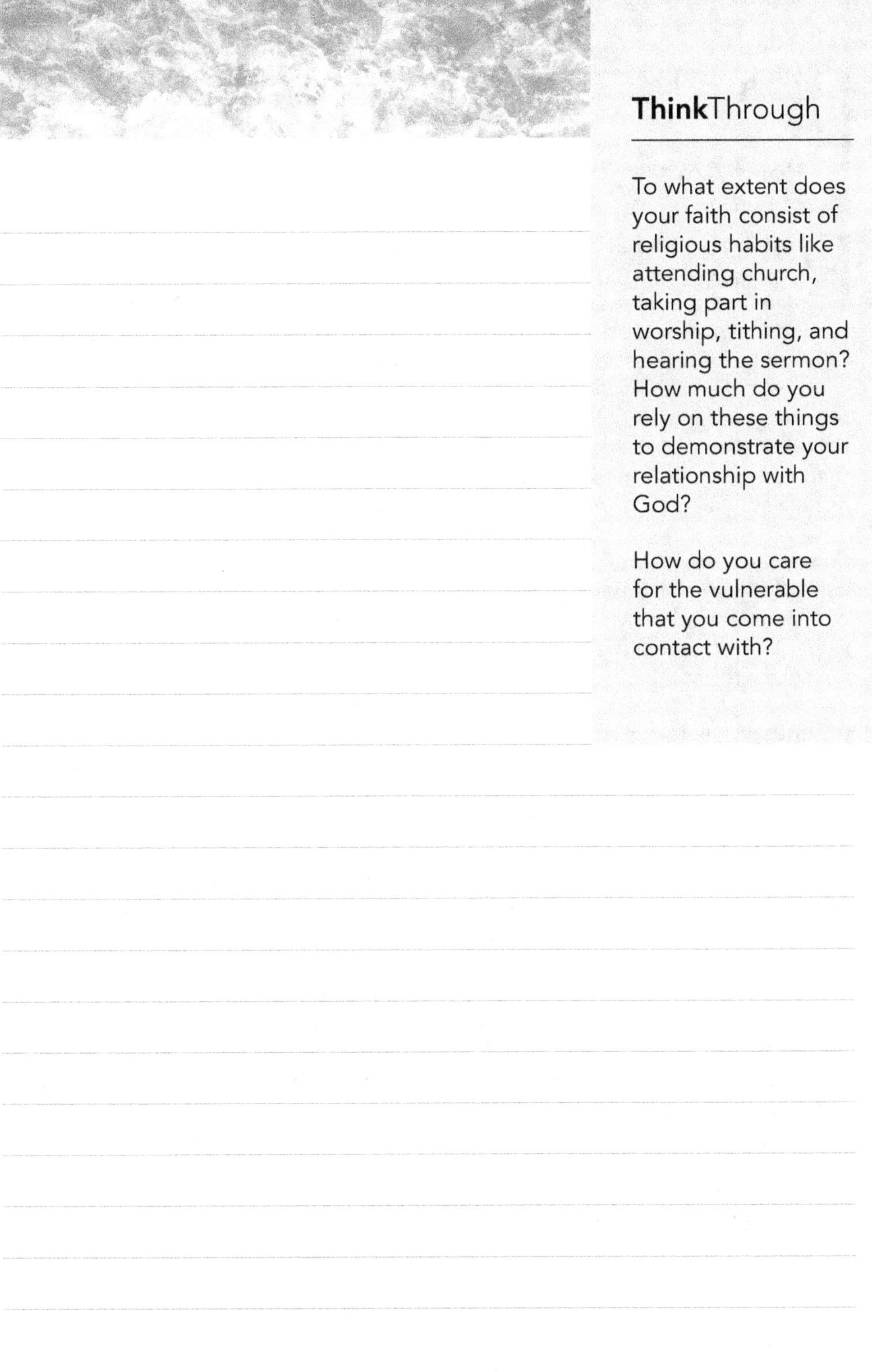


ThinkThrough

To what extent does your faith consist of religious habits like attending church, taking part in worship, tithing, and hearing the sermon? How much do you rely on these things to demonstrate your relationship with God?

How do you care for the vulnerable that you come into contact with?

# Day 18

**Read** Amos 5:25–27

Paintings often have a staggering value assigned to them. Yet many of the famous artists behind them struggled to make a living out of their passion when they were alive. Even though their works now hang in famous galleries and are hailed as examples of pinnacles of the technique, some of these works were not always valued in their time.

Sometimes, however—such as in the case of British artist, Banksy—works of art are immediately recognised as valuable, both in aesthetic as well as monetary terms.

It's nothing new to create items of value and significance. Throughout history, skilled artists have created artwork that is valuable and worthy of appreciation. But, at times, that appreciation can go too far, and too much value (monetary or otherwise) can be ascribed to a work of art.

That is what the Israelites have done. They have made their own idols and ascribed deity to them. Amos 5:26 is a harsh critique of the ludicrous idea of making something and then worshipping it. Yet, it is nothing new. This generation of Israel is doing what their ancestors had done almost immediately upon leaving Egypt many years ago.

When Moses took "too long" to come down from the mountain, the Israelites pressured Aaron to make an idol for them. When he did, they said that it was the god that had brought them out of Egypt (Exodus 32:1–4). Similarly, when Jeroboam was afraid of people travelling to Jerusalem and reuniting the kingdom, he set up shrines in Bethel and Gilgal and had golden calves made and installed there. Then he told the people the same thing the Israelites said: "Here are your gods, Israel, who brought you up out of Egypt" (1 Kings 12:28).

Israel gave the credit for their deliverance to something that their own hands had made. Even simple reflection reveals this to be nonsensical. But the offence goes beyond doing something illogical; they have robbed God of the glory that is due to Him alone, and ascribed it to something else. For this, they will be sent into exile (Amos 5:27). They will be removed from their homes and their land, and sent to a foreign place and be subject to a foreign people. **God takes His glory seriously.**

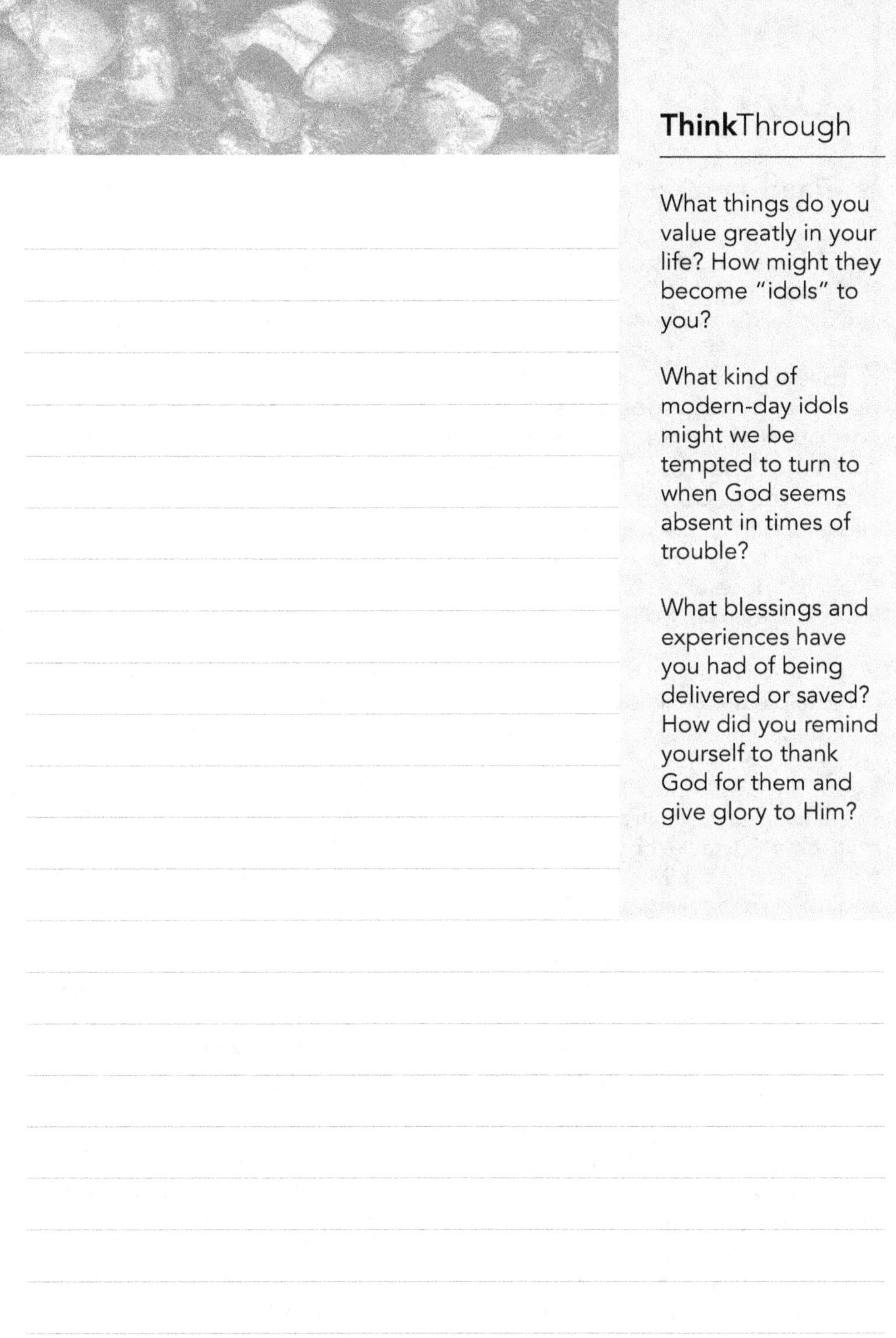

ThinkThrough

What things do you value greatly in your life? How might they become "idols" to you?

What kind of modern-day idols might we be tempted to turn to when God seems absent in times of trouble?

What blessings and experiences have you had of being delivered or saved? How did you remind yourself to thank God for them and give glory to Him?

# **Day** 19



You've probably heard these warnings that what is on the outside may not reflect what is on the inside: "Don't judge a book by its cover", or, "Appearances can be deceiving". **God, too, says that the outside appearance is not what matters, but what is inside that counts.** When Samuel was choosing a new king to replace Saul, God said: "People look at the outward appearance, but the LORD looks at the heart" (1 Samuel 16:7).

In this next "woe" saying, Amos paints a picture of an Israelite society that looks promising on the surface; God appears to be blessing them (Amos 6:1, 3–6). Amos lists some of the luxuries and extravagances that some in Israel—both the northern kingdom (Mount Samaria) and the southern kingdom (Zion)—are enjoying. These people have expensive and ornate furniture (v. 4), eat the choicest foods (v. 4), drink wine by the bowlful (v. 6), enjoy their music (v. 5), and pamper themselves with the finest of lotions (v. 6).

So what? Is it wrong to enjoy a lavish lifestyle? Is it wrong to be rich? The simple answer is no. But we must remember how all of this luxury has been financed. It has been purchased with money taken unjustly from the poor through a corrupt justice system (see 2:6–8). This is highlighted by the final phrase of Amos 6:6: "You do not grieve over the ruin of Joseph." This "ruin" refers to the exploitation of the poor and powerless by the rich. The mention of Joseph, a reference to the southern tribes, is another reminder (see 3:1–2) that in God's design, Israel included the whole house of Israel, not just the 10 northern tribes.

These people were doing what Jesus warned people against when He said that men cannot serve both God and money (Luke 16:13). The Israelites were "worshipping" their money and not God, as implied by the descriptions of opulence in Amos 6:4–6. They were content to pursue their own comfort and had no thought of their neighbour—and very little for God. Worshipping God means loving Him and loving one's neighbour, but the Israelites—while continuing with their worship practices and offerings—were not doing either. Instead, they were treating their neighbour with abuse, extortion, and injustice.

Once again, Amos announces the judgment: the feasting and lounging will end as the people will be taken into exile (Amos 6:7). When that happens, those who are ill-treating the poor and powerless will themselves become the abused and disenfranchised. The haves will become the have-nots.



Reflect on your lifestyle and the things that you are concerned about. How do they compare to your love for God and your neighbour?

Amos accuses the people of being complacent in their apparent security (Amos 6:1). What does complacency look like, and why is it dangerous?

# Day 20

**Read** Amos 6:8–11

There are very few guarantees in life, especially when it comes to circumstances or events. Things are often beyond our control. We may promise others the world, but, at times, find that we cannot follow through on our word.

It goes without saying that these limitations don't apply to God. If He says it, He will do it. He is the perfect example of what Jesus encouraged us to do—"Do not break your oath . . . All you need to say is simply 'Yes,' or 'No'" (see Matthew 5:33–37). So, when we read statements like "The Sovereign Lord has sworn by himself" (Amos 6:8), we should pay attention. God is going out of His way to let Israel (and us as readers) know that He is saying something important.

In Amos 6:9–11, God gives both the indictment (the crimes and sins of Israel) and the discipline that is coming because of it. The new charge against Israel is laid out in synonymous statements that say the same thing in two different ways: God "abhor[s] the pride of Jacob" and "detest[s] his fortresses" (v. 8). The repetition serves to reinforce the point that Israel is relying on herself and not on God. **Israel was guilty of taking pride in her military, which suggests that they not only believed themselves invulnerable, but also credited themselves for their own position and success.**

Their discipline will disabuse them of this pride (vv. 8–9, 11). Their military will not be able to save the city that God is going to destroy (v. 8). He will smash the houses, both great and small, into rubble (v. 11). The picture is one of a city razed to the ground.

This destruction is further elaborated in verses 9 to 10. The punishment extends from a general destruction of homes (v. 11) to a more personal one of individuals being killed—even those who are left and those hiding from the punishment (vv. 9–10). It is so severe that the survivors live in deep fear, unsure about which of their actions will evoke further punishment. They are so bewildered and confused that they dare not even mention the name of the v (v. 10), lest this inadvertently provokes His wrath.

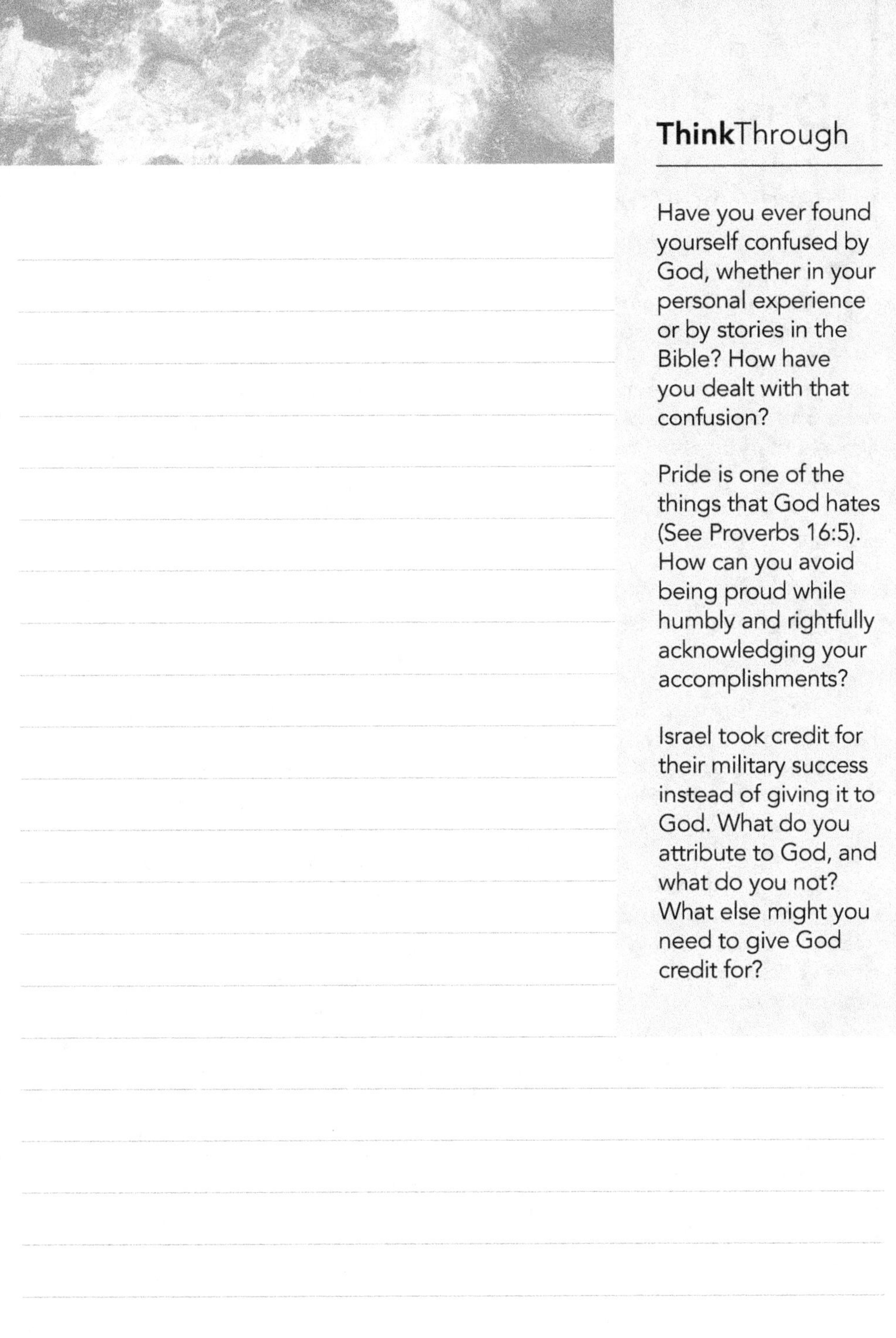



Have you ever found yourself confused by God, whether in your personal experience or by stories in the Bible? How have you dealt with that confusion?

Pride is one of the things that God hates (See Proverbs 16:5). How can you avoid being proud while humbly and rightfully acknowledging your accomplishments?

Israel took credit for their military success instead of giving it to God. What do you attribute to God, and what do you not? What else might you need to give God credit for?

# Day 21

**Read** Amos 6:12–14

Take a moment to think about the strangest thing you have ever seen. Perhaps it was a performance, like a contortionist or an acrobat. Maybe it was a rock formation that looked just like a human face. Or, maybe it was something "out of place", like someone using a brand-new cell phone in a remote village. Imagine something that made you scratch your head and think, *That's not right, that doesn't make sense!*

That's the kind of image Amos uses in Amos 6:12–14. He asks two questions, both of which point to things clearly out of place and which would elicit an obvious "no" in response. To the original hearers, the first image of horses running on rocky cliffs would have been ridiculous, as horses would run on rock-free grounds. The second image is just as ridiculous: the sea doesn't get ploughed, by oxen or any other animal.

But this is exactly what Israel has done in her society. She has turned "justice into poison" and "righteousness into bitterness" (v. 12). Both of these things are things that just do not happen. They are unexpected and confusing, and raise the questions: *What were you thinking? Why would you do that?*

Part of the answer comes in verse 13. We have seen earlier that Israel had forgotten what God had done for them and were taking pride in "their" accomplishments (v. 8). Verse 13 speaks of the same thing: Israel has convinced herself that her military accomplishments were by her own might—though Amos uses a clever play on words here to show them that what they have done (and taken Yahweh's credit for) really amounts to nothing. Believing in our self-sufficiency is not a big step from using everything to our own advantage, including the justice and religious systems. **It becomes easy to assume that nothing is beyond our control and then manipulate what we have at hand to serve our interests.**

So the LORD is going to send discipline to the Israelites (v. 14). This time, however, the discipline is meant to demonstrate something to Israel as well as serve as the consequence for her sins. God is going to "stir up a nation . . . that will oppress you all the way" (v. 14). This will show Israel that God is ultimately behind the success or failure of an army. If they had thought that they had defeated Karnaim by their own strength (v. 13),

they would now learn that their strength would fail, especially when God was behind the other army.



Israel was meant to be a light to the nations (see Genesis 12:1–3), partly by how their society was to be different. In what ways do you live differently so that your life serves as a light to others?

What do you think about God using nations or people as instruments of His discipline? How might this idea change how you see global events?

# Day 22

**Read** Amos 7:1–9

Documentaries on "Behind the Scenes" or "The Making of" give us a glimpse of what we don't normally see in a movie. It could be the eight hours of make-up that it takes to create our favourite superhero, or the special training that actors have to go through to create that realistic fight scene. And most of the time, there's a surprise or two in the peek behind the finished product, when we get to see what went into the making of something.

This is what we are being given in Amos 7:1–9. It is unclear whether or not Amos had communicated this message to his original audience, but it was certainly recorded for later Israelites (and later readers of the Bible) to read. Thus far, we have been reading the messages that Amos delivered to his listeners in Israel. Now, the book turns to recording a visionary interaction between God and Amos.

God continues to show Amos the plans He has for disciplining Israel (Amos 7:1, 4). But this time, Amos intercedes and begs God not to send the planned punishment (vv. 2, 5). We might ask: Did Amos beg God to withhold judgment on previous occasions? If not, why was he doing it now? Was the planned punishment of locusts and fire much more severe than the others? Whatever the reason, it drives Amos to beg for God's mercy. And God relents!

Twice, God shows punishments— punishments that are deserved and that are outlined in the law for Israel's sins (see Deuteronomy 28:15–68)— and twice, on Amos' intercession, God relents (Amos 7:3, 6)

The third vision shows that the discipline is deserved. God is going to set a plumb-line against Israel to show how far she is from what is right (v. 7). This raises the interesting question: If Israel indeed deserved discipline for deviating so far from God's laws, then why did God relent? **Did God hold back because of Amos' prayers?**

Possibly—that is the impression that verses 3 and 6 give. God does go on to say that He will raise His sword against Israel (v. 9), but He will spare them the two particular punishments of locusts and fire. Though the discipline is deserved, God withholds His hand on Amos' request for the safety of his people.

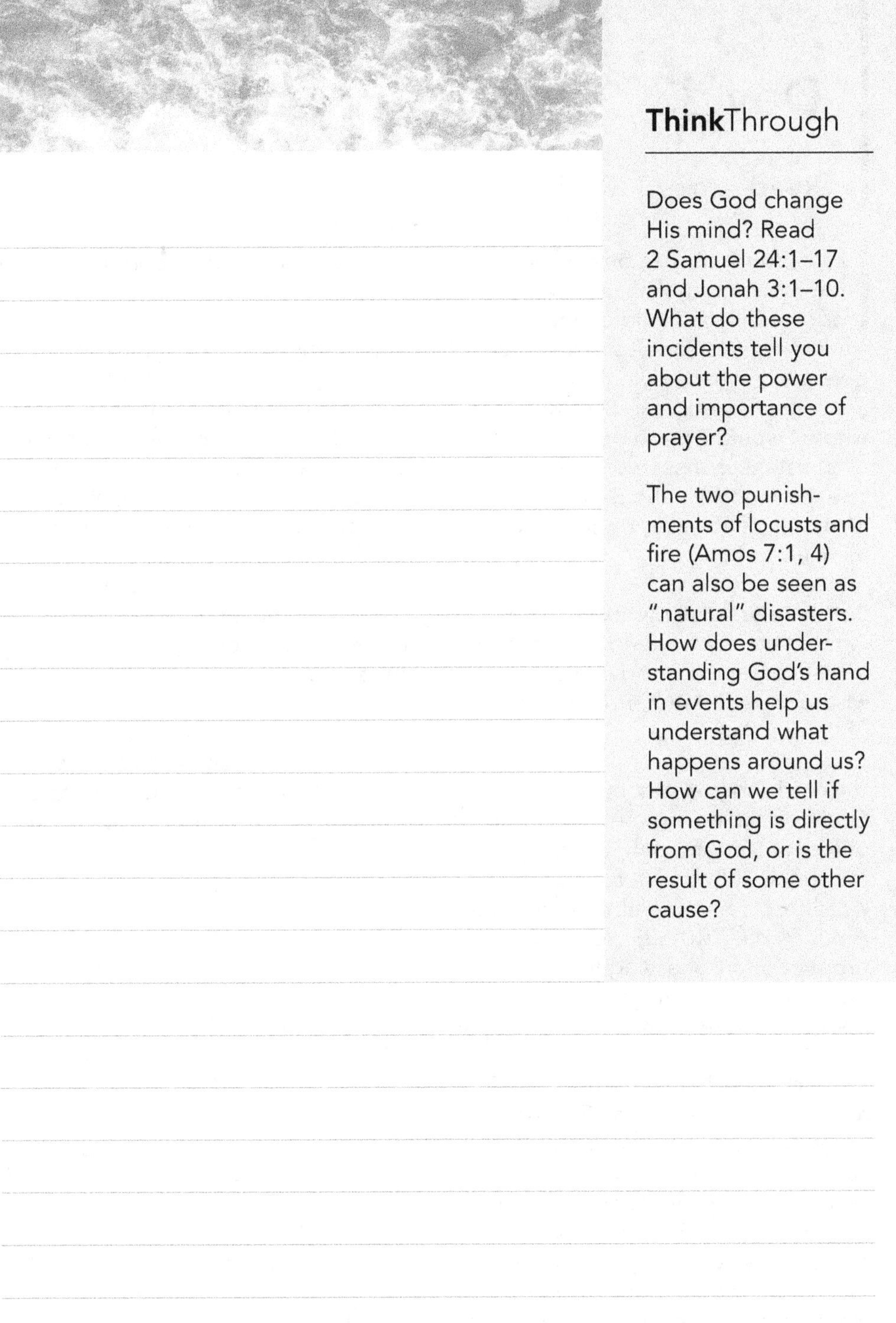

ThinkThrough

Does God change His mind? Read 2 Samuel 24:1–17 and Jonah 3:1–10. What do these incidents tell you about the power and importance of prayer?

The two punishments of locusts and fire (Amos 7:1, 4) can also be seen as "natural" disasters. How does understanding God's hand in events help us understand what happens around us? How can we tell if something is directly from God, or is the result of some other cause?

# Day 23

**Read** Amos 7:10–17

If you could choose one person in the Bible to emulate, who would it be? And if you could choose one situation in the Bible to experience personally, what would it be? There are so many people in Scripture whom I would love to be like and circumstances that I would like to experience, for the Bible is full of stories of amazing people and miraculous things.

But there are also plenty of things in the Bible that I would not want to have experienced, and some people whose shoes I'd rather not be in. One of them is Amos.

Unsurprisingly, Amos' message about God's discipline has met a fair amount of resistance. Amaziah, the priest of the shrine at Bethel (a false place of worship, if you remember) confronts Amos (Amos 7:10–13). He accuses the prophet of prophesying for financial gain and tells him to go peddle his wares elsewhere (vv. 12–13).

As he did earlier (3:8), Amos' responds by stating that God has called him to prophesy, and he cannot do anything other than relate the message from God to his audience (7:14–15). In other words, Amos is saying that this is not his idea, and these are not his words. He is God's spokesman, and what he says comes directly from God. Then he tells Amaziah that God has a word just for him (v. 17).

This is why I would want to avoid being in Amos' shoes. Imagine having to look into someone's eyes and tell him that his wife is going to become a prostitute, his children are going to be murdered, his land and possessions will be taken away from him, and he will die in a foreign land (v. 17). That is a hard message to deliver. Yet Amos obediently delivers such a personal prophecy to Amaziah.

God has spoken, what else can Amos do? **A prophet is only a prophet when he delivers the message God has given him.**

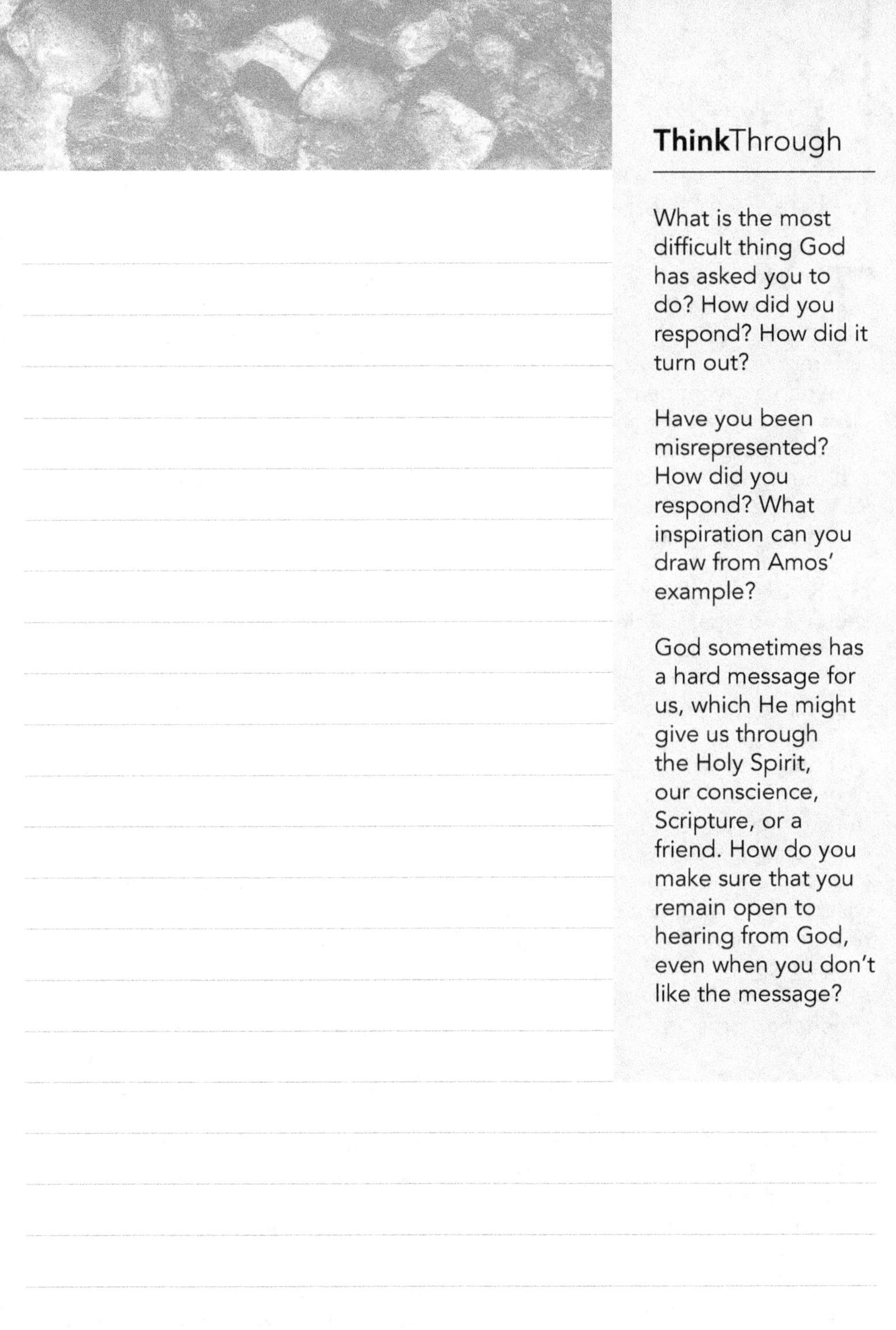



What is the most difficult thing God has asked you to do? How did you respond? How did it turn out?

Have you been misrepresented? How did you respond? What inspiration can you draw from Amos' example?

God sometimes has a hard message for us, which He might give us through the Holy Spirit, our conscience, Scripture, or a friend. How do you make sure that you remain open to hearing from God, even when you don't like the message?

# Day 24

**Read** Amos 8:1–3

Timing is everything. God's timeline is often vastly different from ours and certainly different from what we would choose if we had a say in the matter. But God's timing is just right. We know that Jesus came into the world at just the right time (see Galatians 4:4, Romans 5:6). And He will come back at just the right time.

In this next vision (Amos 8:1–3), God shows Amos that the time has come for Israel to be judged. The prophet is shown a basket of ripe fruit, fruit that is just right to be consumed. Just as the time is right to eat the fruit, the time is right to judge the people of Israel. God will "spare them no longer" (v. 2). This phrase connects this vision with that of the plumb-line, when God also said, "I will spare them no longer" (7:8). This repetition shows the consistency of Amos' message to God's people and reinforces the certainty of his prophetic words.

There is another repeated idea in this section of Amos. It is a phrase that has been used a number of times previously as well: Amos refers to God as "the Sovereign Lord" (8:1, 3). This is something that should not be dismissed as merely a title. When Amos refers to God as "the Sovereign Lord," he is reminding the people to whom they actually belong. God is the one who gives and takes life; He is the one who orders the sun and moon to their places and calls the stars out by name (Psalm 19:1–6; 147:4). He is the one who feeds the lion (Psalm 104:20–21), and causes the lilies of the fields to bloom (Matthew 6:28). He is, as Paul would later write to the church in Colossae, the creator and sustainer of life (Colossians 1:15–20; see also Amos 5:8).

All the historical references in the book of Amos, from the exodus (2:10; 3:1) and the battles (2:9) to the covenant (2:4), were meant to remind the people of God's power and provision. They were to remind them of His right—and His responsibility—to hold Israel accountable for her actions. **So when the Sovereign Lord declares that the time has come, the time has indeed come.**

That time will turn songs of worship into wailing, and the devastation caused by the judgment of God will leave people speechless (8:3). We often say, "I don't know what to say"—yet speak anyway. But on the day when God's judgment is visited upon His people, the magnitude of the death and carnage will render people silent. Bodies will be "flung everywhere" (v. 3). God's prophesied judgment will be thorough and complete. This dire warning is meant to call people to repentance and faithfulness to God.



The picture painted by Amos of God in Amos 8:1–3 seems rather vengeful. How does it compare with other pictures of God in Scripture? How would you reconcile these differences?

Amos reminds us that God is sovereign, and nothing happens outside His control. What questions might this truth prompt you to ask in difficult circumstances? And what hope might it offer?

# **Day** 25

**Read** Amos 8:4–8

In biblical studies, students are frequently told to watch for repetition. If something is repeated, it means that it is likely to be pretty important. The Israelites' treatment of the poor and the needy was obviously a very important feature of his prophecy.

In Amos 8:4–8, Amos returns to images that he used in his very first accusation against Israel. In fact, he uses the exact same language to point out Israel's failure in being a just society according to God's way. They were trampling on the needy and poor (2:7, 8:4), and buying and selling the poor for silver or a pair of sandals (2:6, 8:6).

Here in chapter 8, he adds some new details. So great is the greed that drives the Israelites, that they cannot wait for their religious festivals to be over so they can resume their dishonest market practices in order to make more money (v. 5). This is the epitome of what Jesus said about being unable to serve God and money (Luke 16:13). **While loving God does not necessarily mean we need to hate money, loving money can translate into hating God, in that we no longer honour and obey God's ways.**

All they want to do is to return to their shops so they can get more money for as little work as possible—which they achieve with the use of dishonest scales and selling "the sweepings with the wheat" (Amos 8:6).

It is after this revelation of the specifics of the Israelites' dishonest business practices, that one of the most startling statements of the book of Amos comes. God has said that there will be drastic and severe punishment for their sins—that people will be taken into exile and that bodies would be thrown out through breaches in the walls (4:2–3, 5:27)—but nothing is as stark as what He says now: "I will never forget anything they have done" (8:7).

God is omniscient. It is impossible for Him to forget anything. But this is especially terrifying in the context of sin and judgment. If God will not forget what He has seen them do, and always remembers Israel's guilt, this means His judgment upon them will be inescapable.

If you are anything like me, there are likely to be a good number of things you've done that you would like God to forget. Or, at least, you wouldn't want Him to see you as guilty. Fortunately, unlike the Israelites in

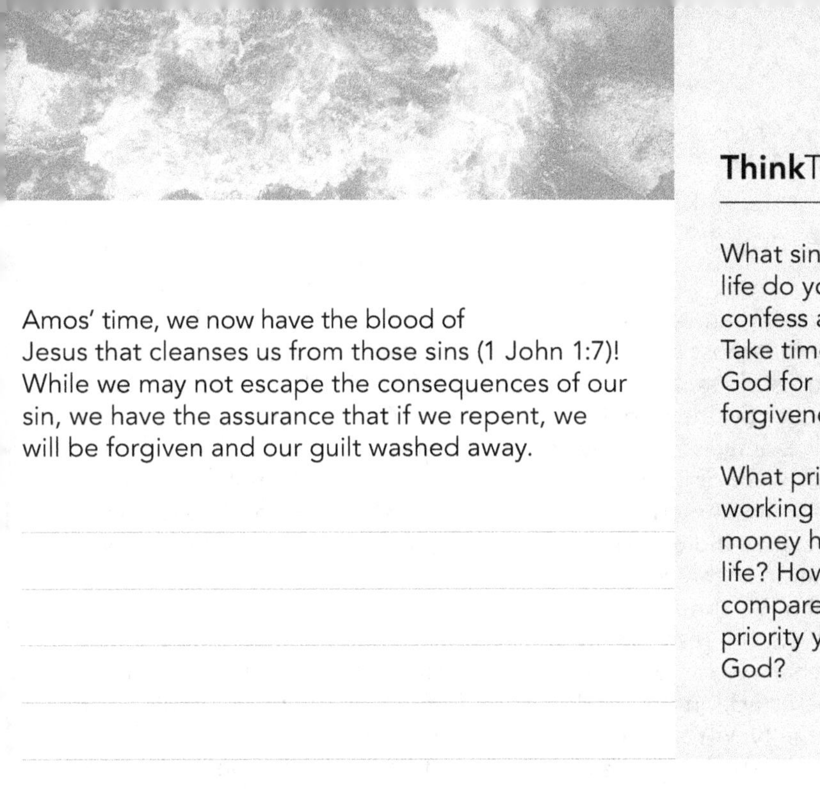

Amos' time, we now have the blood of
Jesus that cleanses us from those sins (1 John 1:7)!
While we may not escape the consequences of our
sin, we have the assurance that if we repent, we
will be forgiven and our guilt washed away.



What sin in your
life do you need to
confess and repent?
Take time to thank
God for His gift of
forgiveness.

What priority does
working and earning
money have in your
life? How does it
compare to the
priority you give to
God?

# **Day** 26

**Read** Amos 8:9–10

There are certain events in history that most people would remember. Even if it didn't affect them directly, they would be able to recall exactly where they were and what they were doing when it occurred. For many Americans in the United States, it would be events like the assassination of the country's President John F. Kennedy on 22 November 1963, the resignation of President Richard Nixon on 9 August 1974, and the attack on the World Trade Center in New York on 11 September 2001. These are days that live in infamy in Americans' collective and individual memory.

There are also days that we anticipate with overwhelming excitement— like the first day of a new job, our wedding day, moving into one's first home, the birth of a child, or a long-awaited retirement.

There is a day in Scripture that is like that too, a day which everyone looks towards, some with great anticipation and others with great trepidation. It is the "day of the Lord", often referred to as "that day" (Amos 8:9). Amos mentions it many times (see, for example, 2:16; 5:18, 20; 8:3, 13), and each mention is in reference to a day of punishment, sadness, sorrow, destruction, and death.

Amos isn't the only prophet to mention this day. Isaiah, Ezekiel, Joel, Obadiah, Zephaniah, Zechariah, and Malachi all refer to it in the Old Testament. It is also mentioned in Acts, 1 and 2 Corinthians, 1 and 2 Thessalonians, and 2 Peter in the New Testament. It is also likely alluded to in Revelation.

The "day of the Lord" refers to a time when God intervenes directly in human history to accomplish some part of His overarching goal, for both good and punishment. Many of the references can be understood to point to an event (or series of events) that will take place at the end of human history, just before the consummation of God's kingdom. But there are also interim "days of the Lord" when God sends discipline on His people to call them back to covenant faithfulness.

The "day of the Lord" is a day to be feared. It is a day of darkness and mourning. It will be a day of great loss, like the loss of an only son (v. 10). It is a day that will be remembered by those who experience it. **No one will miss it or forget it when God visits His people.**

ThinkThrough

What are your own feelings towards the "day of the LORD" or "that day" (Amos 8:9)? Why do you feel that way?

What good things will happen on that day? (see Isaiah 4:2; 10:20, 27; 11:10–11; 28:5; 29:18)

When has God intervened in your life? How did you respond, and how did they affect your faith and walk with God?

**Read** Amos 8:11–14

Survivalist shows were extremely popular on TV at one point. These shows, which depicted humans battling nature and the elements, tapped into a primal survival urge in many people. They showed people living in the extreme conditions north of the Arctic circle, giving up modern amenities to return to a "simpler" way of life, or being thrust into the wilderness with a limited selection of tools.

One thing that was stressed and repeated in these show was the listing of the essentials for survival: shelter, food, water, and warmth. With these basic needs met, it was said, a person could survive indefinitely.

Amos—and Jesus—would disagree. When Jesus was hungry after fasting for 40 days in the wilderness, Satan tempted Him to turn stones into bread (see Matthew 4:1–3). Jesus' famous reply was: "Man shall not live on bread alone, but on every word that comes from the mouth of God" (v. 4). **Jesus was intimating that man could go on longer without bread, but not as long without the Word of God.**

In Amos 8:11–14, Amos tells Israel that God is going to withhold this vital element of life. Unlike a famine of food or water (v. 11), which were part of the covenant curses found in Deuteronomy 28:22–24, this famine will be one of the very thing that Jesus said that people cannot live without—the word of the LORD (Amos 8:11). The people will not hear God's voice. They will not hear or know the law, nor will they receive any message of wisdom, guidance, hope, or assurance from Him. This drought will leave even the youngest and strongest weak and staggering (v. 12).

This seems to be the case of not knowing what you are missing until it is gone. The people of Israel have not been listening to nor depending on God's words. And now, they will no longer have His words.

This is a strange punishment. It seems as though God is going to withhold the one thing that Israel would need to find their way back to Him. What would the people need more during a time of punishment and exile, than to hear again the word of the LORD calling them to repentance and covenant faithfulness? But all they will hear is the silence of their own sinfulness.

How important is the Word of God to you? Do you miss it when it is not a part of your life?

What would you do if you suddenly did not have access to the words and story of God?

# Day 28

**Read** Amos 9:1–6

It can sometimes be hard to tell the difference between the most dramatic point of a story and its conclusion, between its climax and its resolution. The climax of the story is when the major conflict is finally decided—for example, who wins and who loses in a war. But after that happens, there may be some plot details that still need resolution. For example, what happens to the winners and the losers after the battle is over? Where do they go, and what do they do?

Some people think the story is over once they see the climax, and are not interested in the resolution. But both can be equally important.

Imagine if Jesus died on the cross but did not rise from the dead, ascend into heaven, or promise to return. The climax would still be significant: the new covenant would begin and a way to forgive sins would be offered to all. But there would be no life everlasting, no future with Jesus, no reunion with all those who have gone before. A climax removes the obstacles; a resolution solves the problems.

In Amos 9, over the next three days' readings, we will reach both the climax and resolution of Amos' prophetic work. The first 10 verses (today's and tomorrow's reading) give the longest description of punishment found in the book of Amos. Here, the punishment serves both as a description of the coming fate of Israel as well as a theology lesson for her.

Amos 9:1–6 describes the extent to which God will go to discipline His people for their sins. No one will escape it (v. 1), and there is nowhere that Israel can go or hide from God (vv. 2–4). This is a demonstration of God's omnipresence. It is a contrast from the description of God in Psalm 139, in which He is watching over His people to guard and protect. In Amos 9, God is keeping His "eye on them for harm and not for good" (v. 4).

Amos 9:5–6, meanwhile, speak of God's limitless power—His omnipotence. God's power is on full display here: His mere touch melts the earth (v. 5), and His palace, where He reigns, extends from earth to the heavens (v. 6). **This is a picture of a sovereign God who rules everything and has both the right and the power to execute His will.**

This is the climax. God has the right, the power, and the reason to execute His punishment on Israel. Of its certainty and extent there can be no doubt, because "the Lord is his name" (v. 6).

Has there ever been a time when you doubted God's power? Why did you doubt? What role does doubt play in your life of faith?

There is comfort in the fact that we cannot outrun God, even when it concerns His judgment. Has there been a time when you felt that God was not near? How did you remind yourself of His presence?

Amos 9:1–6 paint a picture of God being in control of everything, from natural forces to invading armies. What circumstances remind you that God is in control, even when things seem out of control?

**Read** Amos 9:7–10

Israel seems to have had a historical problem with identity. We have seen how they relied on the fact that they were God's chosen people to brush off the accusations and warnings that Amos was delivering (see 3:1–2). In Jesus' day, the Israelites also claimed their special status and relationship to God, but John the Baptist warned them not to think they could escape punishment because of their heritage (Matthew 3:9).

Amos has a startling wake-up call for them too. While he had earlier noted the special relationship between Israel and God (Amos 3:2)—and also stressed that this meant a greater responsibility, not just greater favour—he now tells the Israelites that to God, they are no different from the Cushites, the Philistines, and the Arameans (9:7). This is perhaps the most shocking statement in all of the book of Amos. Yet, it may also be the most necessary.

**If Israel were ever to find their way again, they need to know exactly who God is and who they are.** Since they are no different from the other nations, God will discipline them for their sins— they will suffer the same conclusion as the nations surrounding Israel do in Amos 1:3–2:3. God will destroy the sinful kingdom of Israel (9:8). This is the climax of all that has been building up in the prophecy of Amos: the end of the kingdom of Israel.

At this point, you might ask: What about God's promises to Abraham and David (Genesis 17:4–8; 2 Samuel 7:8–13)? Surely God will not abandon His people entirely?

Remember, however, that the climax is not the resolution. There is still a resolution to this story, as God immediately begins to tie up the loose ends: "Yet I will not totally destroy the descendants of Jacob" (Amos 9:8).

Right after announcing the punishment, God immediately speaks of the remnant that will be left. The guilty will be punished and will perish, but God will save those who have been the victims of Israel's greed—remember the innocent for whom justice has been turned into bitterness (5:7, 6:12)? Still, while the innocent will be spared, they will have to go through the punishment that is slated for the guilty (see 9:9–10 on the guilty perishing by the sword). They will find themselves in other countries, away from the land that God had promised to Abraham, Isaac, and Jacob (vv. 4, 9).

This turn towards resolution answers the questions about the fate of the poor, needy, and innocent. It answers the questions about God's love for His people and His pledges to Israel's ancestors about being their God. He is a God of justice and fairness.



Sometimes, it seems that the innocent victims of a certain sin are caught up in the punishment for the perpetrators. What do you think of this?

Sometimes, God may be doing something that is bigger than our individual circumstances. How can you remind yourself of this?

In Amos 9:7, God compares Israel to the Philistines and the Arameans to remind them that He is the God of all humanity, not just Israel. How does knowing that God is the one true God help you engage with people who do not believe in Him?

# **Day** 30



Many of us grow up on stories that end "happily ever after". However, once we've had some life experience, we discover that finding a good, happy resolution is not as simple as we once believed. Amid the difficulties of life, trying to end a story happily takes a lot of work, patience, apologies, and forgiveness.

But the resolution that follows the climax of Amos' prophecies tells us that there really is a "happily ever after". After the many chapters of Israel's sin and God's judgment, the book of Amos ends with the beautiful picture of Israel's future.

Coming back to "that day" (Amos 9:11), Amos now describes not death and destruction, but life more abundant than one can imagine. God will not only restore Israel to her land (v. 15), but will also rebuild her walls, and bless her crops (v. 11, 13–14). And all this will be done by God himself. The many references to "I" in these verses are significant, just as they were in the sections on judgment. God is not present in discipline and distant in blessing; rather, He is active among His people at all times, both in consequence and in reward.

God himself paints a picture of an Israel so abundant with life that they cannot keep up with its produce (v. 13).

The people will still be eating the fruits of the previous harvest when the time comes to plant. This abundant fertility is coupled with peace with their neighbours (as shown by them being able to plant vineyards, live in cities, and not be uprooted). Not only will they enjoy abundant harvests, but they will also be able to enjoy the fruit of their vines and the crops of their fields in peace and safety.

And, amazingly, this is not even the greatest blessing of the resolution.

Throughout his prophetic speeches, Amos has been speaking the words of the LORD to Israel and reminding them that it is the LORD who has spoken. Until now, he has been referring to God as "the LORD," "the Sovereign LORD," "the LORD God Almighty," or "the LORD Almighty". Here, right at the end, Amos refers to Him as "the LORD *your* God" (v. 15). **The ultimate resolution is not restoration to prosperity, but restoration to a relationship with the God who chose them.**

ThinkThrough

How will you wait
for the coming day
when all things
are made right
and God's reign
is full and final?
What activities will
become important
as you think about
the fullness of God's
kingdom? How will
you pray about it?

Is there a particular
aspect of the com-
ing kingdom that
you are anticipating
most? What is it and
why?

# Journey Through
# Hosea

As God's spokesman, Hosea is told by Him to marry Gomer, a prostitute, and to go again and again to woo her back despite her many infidelities. Hosea's commitment to love Gomer gives us a glimpse of God's love for us. God loves His people as passionately and as jealously as a devoted husband loves his wife. Even when we wander from Him and our hearts cool towards Him, He continues to come after us and to draw us back to Him. God's love will never let us go. Rekindle your love and commitment to the One who loves you!

**David Gibb** is the former Vicar of St. Andrew's Church in Leyland and Honorary Canon of Blackburn Cathedral. He is committed to training church planters and gospel workers, and is one of the contributors to a new NIV Study Bible. He is also author of a book on Revelation.

# Journey Through
# Judges

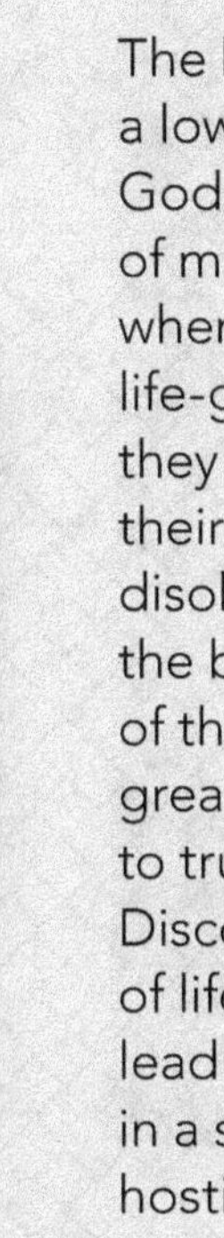


The book of Judges describes a low point in the history of God's people. It tells of a time of moral and spiritual anarchy, when everyone ignored God's life-giving laws and did what they thought was right in their own eyes. It is a story of disobedience and defeat. Yet the book also contains glimpses of the Israelites' capacity for greatness—when they chose to trust and depend on God. Discover God's great principles of life, and find out how we can lead powerful, productive lives in a society that is increasingly hostile to our faith.

**Gary Inrig** is a graduate of the University of British Columbia and Dallas Theological Seminary. An established Bible teacher and former pastor, he has authored several books, including *True North, The Parables, Forgiveness,* and *Whole Marriages in a Broken World.*

# Journey Through

# Ezra & Nehemiah

While they document the historical fulfilment of God's promise that Israel will return home after 70 years of captivity in Babylon, the books of Ezra and Nehemiah offer relevant lessons for us today. We learn about the priority of worship, the centrality of God's Word, and the necessity of witnessing to the world by obeying God. Journey through Ezra-Nehemiah to discover how we can be holy and separate from the sinful world while still being effective witnesses to it.

**Robert M. Solomon** served as Bishop of The Methodist Church in Singapore from 2000–2012. He has an active itinerant preaching and teaching ministry in Singapore and abroad. He is the author of more than 40 books, including *Faithful to the End*, *God in Pursuit*, *Growing Old Gracefully*, and *Raising the Next Generation*.

# Thirsting for more?

Check out **journeythrough.org**

- **Find titles available**
- **Explore other formats:**
Read online or order a print copy

# ABOUT THE PUBLISHER

Discovery House Publishing™
produces a wide array of premium
and quality resources that focus on Scripture,
show reverence for God and His Word,
demonstrate the relevance of vibrant faith,
and equip and encourage you to draw closer
to God in all seasons of your life.

Discovery House
Publishing™

# NOTE TO THE READER

We invite you to share your response to the message
of this book by writing to us at:

**5 Pereira Road #07-01
Asiawide Industrial Building
Singapore 368025**

or sending an email to:

**dhpsingapore@dhp.org**